95

Ruth Bader Ginsburg

Fire and Steel on the Supreme Court

RUTH BADER GINSBURG
FIRE AND STEEL
ON THE SUPREME COURT

by

ELEANOR H. AYER

A People in Focus Book

DILLON PRESS
New York

Maxwell Macmillan Canada
Toronto

Maxwell Macmillan International
New York   Oxford   Singapore   Sydney

Acknowledgments

My sincere appreciation to Toni House, Public Information Officer at the Supreme Court of the United States, for her multifaceted assistance on this project. I am also grateful to Justice Ruth Bader Ginsburg for reading the manuscript prior to publication and offering comments to correct or clarify the text.

Photo Credits

Cover: Richard W. Strauss, Smithsonian Institution, Courtesy of the Supreme Court of the United States.
6: AP/Wide World Photos. 11-15: "Collection of the Supreme Court of the United States." 16: AP/Wide World Photos. 18-50: "Collection of the Supreme Court of the United States." 56-60: AP/Wide World Photos. 62-67: "Collection of the Supreme Court of the United States." 76-102: AP/Wide World Photos.

Book design by Carol Matsuyama

Library of Congress Cataloging-in-Publication Data

Ayer, Eleanor H.
    Ruth Bader Ginsburg : fire and steel on the Supreme Court / by Eleanor H. Ayer. — 1st ed.
        p. cm. — (A People in focus book)
    Includes bibliographical references and index.
    ISBN 0-87518-651-3
    1. Ginsburg, Ruth Bader—Juvenile literature. 2. Judges—United States—Biography—Juvenile literature. 3. United States. Supreme Court—Biography—Juvenile literature. [1. Ginsburg, Ruth Bader. 2. Judges. 3. United States. Supreme Court—Biography. 4. Women—Biography.] I. Title. II. Series.
    KF8745.G56A94 1994
    347.73'2634—dc20
    [B]
    [347.3073534]
    [B]   94-17854

A biography of the second female Supreme Court justice, describing her battle for equal rights for members of both sexes.

Dillon Press   Maxwell Macmillan Canada, Inc.
Macmillan Publishing Company   1200 Eglinton Avenue East
866 Third Avenue   Suite 200
New York, NY 10022   Don Mills, Ontario M3C 3N1

Macmillan Publishing Company is part of the Maxwell Communication Group of Companies.

First edition

Printed in the United States of America

10 9 8 7 6 5 4 3 2 1

/Contents

President Bill Clinton stands beside Ruth Bader Ginsburg in the White House Rose Garden on June 14, 1993, the day he nominated her to be the 107th justice of the Supreme Court.

Chapter / One

"I Pray That I May Be All That She Would Have Been"

June 14, 1993, was a gorgeous, sunny day in the White House Rose Garden, just outside the president's Oval Office. Through the years, many presidential receptions and special events had been held here. Britain's Queen Elizabeth II was honored at a state dinner; former President Nixon's daughter Tricia was married to Edward Cox in a ceremony here. Now, on this Monday, President Bill Clinton stood in the Rose Garden beside the woman he would nominate to be the 107th justice of the Supreme Court of the United States.

As friends, family, and members of Congress listened, the president explained why he had chosen Ruth Bader Ginsburg for this important post. In her years as a judge, said Clinton, she had "distinguished herself as one of our nation's best judges, progressive in outlook, wise in judgment, balanced

and fair in her opinions." The president talked of
Judge Ginsburg's "pioneering work in behalf of the
women of this country," recalling her many years as
a lawyer in the field of women's rights.

Nominating a justice to the nation's highest
court "is one of the most significant duties assigned
to the President," Clinton explained. That person,
along with the eight other justices on the Court,
"decides the most significant questions of our time
and shapes the continuing contours of our liber-
ty. . . . I know well how the Supreme Court affects
the lives of all Americans personally and deeply."[1]

President Clinton's nomination of Judge Ginsburg did not ensure that she actually would sit on
the Court. Before she could become a justice, she
would have to be confirmed by the U.S. Senate.
First, a select group of senators would look into
Ginsburg's past, ask her questions about her views
on certain issues, and decide if she were fit for the
job. They would then pass their recommendation
on to the full Senate.

Throughout the president's short speech, Ruth
Ginsburg's face showed a small smile—a somewhat
unusual expression for this normally serious, stu-
dious woman. At the conclusion of his address, she
said, "Mr. President, I am grateful beyond measure
for the confidence you have placed in me, and I will
strive with all that I have to live up to your expec-

tations in making this appointment." If confirmed, she would work "to the best of my ability for the advancement of the law in the service of society."

Ginsburg then introduced the members of her family who were with her on this special day. Among them were her son, James, her son-in-law, George T. Spera Jr., and her husband, Martin, "who has been, since our teen-age years, my best friend and biggest booster." She acknowledged Hillary Rodham Clinton, whom she had met for the second time that day. But, she explained, "I am not the first member of my family to stand close to her." At that point, she produced a picture of the First Lady leading members of a New York nursery school class in singing "The Toothbrush Song." At the front of the group was Ginsburg's granddaughter, Clara.

In closing her acceptance speech, Ruth Ginsburg added a thank-you to her mother, Celia Amster Bader, "the bravest and strongest person I have known, who was taken from me much too soon. I pray that I may be all that she would have been had she lived in an age when women could aspire and achieve and daughters are cherished as much as sons."[2] The tribute brought tears to President Clinton's eyes.

To those who knew her well, the style of Judge Ginsburg's speech came as a surprise. For such a private, reserved person, it was out of character for her to make such a personal address. But it was a beautiful way to begin, to show the country that this woman of such outstanding educational and professional achievement also had a very human side.

The mother whom she honored in the Rose Garden speech gave birth to Ruth on March 15, 1933, in Brooklyn, New York. Although her birth certificate listed her as Joan Ruth, throughout her life she would be known as Ruth Joan Bader. Ruth's father, Nathan Bader, was a manufacturer of fur coats and later worked in various clothing stores. The world into which Ruth was born discriminated against Jews and against women—and she was both. Yet that injustice was the spark that would later drive her to great accomplishments in the field of women's rights.

The early 1930s were not particularly prosperous times. With the United States in the middle of the Great Depression, millions of people were out of work and out of hope. In Europe, Adolf Hitler had become Germany's new chancellor just two months before Ruth was born. In the next twelve years, Hitler would lead the entire world into war, and the Jews of Europe into near extinction as a result of the Holocaust. But from that war would

Ruth Joan Bader, aged two

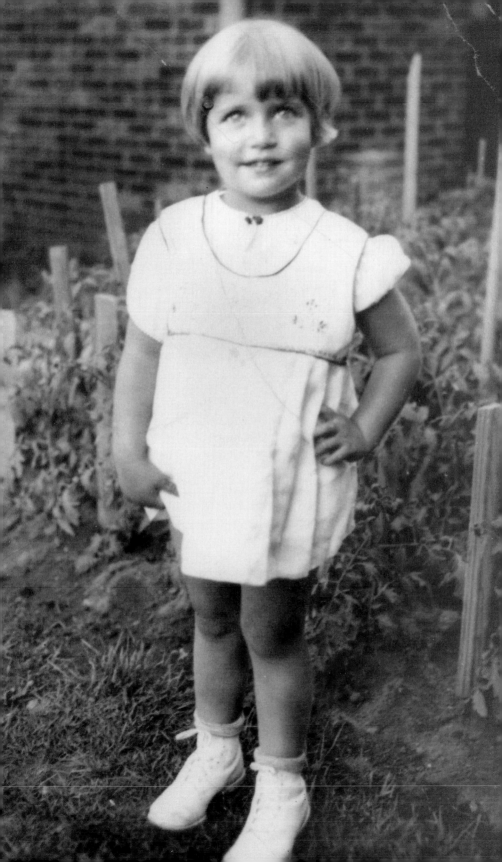

emerge a new respect for women's contributions in the workplace, as well as a sobering horror of the ends to which racial prejudice can lead.

Young Ruth was known to her friends as "Kiki," a nickname given to her by her older sister, Marilyn. Sadly, the sisters had little time together, for at the age of six, Marilyn died of meningitis. Perhaps because he had lost his first daughter, the warm, caring Nathan Bader doted on Ruth and would have spoiled her, she says, had her mother allowed it.

But Celia Bader wanted her daughter to grow up to be an achiever and an independant woman. Discipline, she believed, was an important ingredient of success. An avid reader and a good student, Celia had graduated from high school when she was just fifteen. But because her family had little money, she went to work in New York City's garment district after graduation so her older brother could attend Cornell University. Poverty would deny Celia a college education, but it would not stop her from reading and studying on her own throughout her life.

Some of Ruth's earliest memories are of visiting the public library off Kings Highway in Brooklyn. There, amid the smells of Chinese food from the restaurant one floor below, she and her mother would pore through books of every sort, creating in

Young Ruth with her "double" cousin, Richard Bader. They are doubles because their mothers were sisters and their fathers were brothers.

Ruth an enjoyment of reading that lasted a lifetime.

Along with a love of reading, Celia Bader stressed to her daughter the importance of achievement. In her own time, it was shameful to a husband for his wife to have a job, and thus Celia never worked outside the home. But she encouraged her daughter to be independent and to develop her talents and strengths to the fullest. Her mother's strong character made a deep impression on Ruth and later guided her through the most challenging and difficult obstacles of her career.

Neither at Public School 238 nor later at James Madison High School in Brooklyn did Ruth's friends see many signs of her becoming a feminist or a lawyer. At PS 238, she edited a student publication called *Highway Herald*, for which she wrote an article on the meaning of the Magna Carta, the "Great Charter" of England that later influenced the people who wrote the United States Constitution. The *Herald* also ran a story by Ruth about the Bill of Rights. But there were few other signs that this girl would eventually become one of the leading lawyers in the nation.

"Kiki" Bader was blond and pretty, quiet but well liked for her kind heart and her undisputed intelligence. Richard Salzman, a classmate at James Madison High and now a judge on the District of Columbia Superior Court, says, "Her talent has

Ruth Bader in 1948, speaking to a congregation at Camp Che-Na-Wah, where she was the camp "rabbi."

RUTH BADER
1584 East 9th Street
Arista, Treas. of Go-Getters, School
Orchestra, Twirlers, Sec. to English
Department Chairman, Feature Ed-
itor Term Newspaper
Cornell University

Ruth's entry in her high school yearbook in 1950

been there for anyone to see forever." Ruth's best friend in high school, Ann Burkhardt Kittner, agrees. "She was very modest, and didn't appear to be super self-confident. She never thought she did well on tests, but, of course, she always aced them."[3]

Ruth was far from a bookworm, however. As an active member and treasurer of the Go-Getters, a pep club for the sports teams, Ruth wore a black satin jacket with gold letters and sold tickets to football games. Though an accomplished baton twirler at James Madison, she chipped her tooth at the game against Lincoln High. Certain summers she spent at Camp Che-Na-Wah, in the Adirondack Mountains of northern New York.

Despite her popularity, Ruth Bader was a private person who talked little about personal matters, even among her closest friends. One of the things that she kept to herself was her mother's illness. In 1946, when Ruth was a high school freshman, her mother developed cancer of the cervix. Despite the catastrophic illness, Celia Bader continued to push her daughter to work hard and to achieve. Knowing that she loved to see her studying, Ruth would often sit by Celia's bed at night, doing homework while her mother rested.

For four years, Celia Bader battled the illness. But in June 1950, one day before Ruth's high school graduation, the forty-seven-year-old woman whom her daughter called "very strong, in every way but physical,"[4] died of cancer. It was a devastating blow to Ruth, who was supposed to speak at the graduation ceremony the next day. Instead, teachers brought to her home the many medals she had earned, awards of which her mother would have been very proud.

Years later, when Ruth was asked what event was most responsible for her choosing a career in law, she explained that no single incident had struck her "like a thunderbolt." It was a person—her mother—who had most influenced her career. Celia Bader did not push her daughter to study law. "She was not a career woman," Ruth explained, ". . . but she had tremendous intellect."[5] This intelligent, independent person, who lived in the wrong age for a woman to develop her potential, became the model on which Ruth Bader would pattern herself and her career.

Ruth during her college days at Cornell University. "I did not think of myself as a feminist in the 1950s."

Chapter / Two

The Sting of Being a Woman

She was pretty. She was popular. And, remembered fellow college student Irma Hilton, she was "scary smart."[1]

In the fall of 1950, still struggling to recover from the pain of her mother's death, Ruth Bader left Brooklyn to attend Cornell University in Ithaca, New York. Top grades in high school had earned her a New York State scholarship as well as financial help from the university. Because it interested her very much, she majored in government. But at this point, Ruth had no plans to study law.

Alpha Epsilon Phi, one of two Jewish sororities on campus, accepted her as a member. With the other sorority sisters, Ruth enjoyed dances and teas, parties, and sporting events. Like most universities in the 1950s, Cornell had different social rules for women than for men. Women (but not men) had to wear raincoats over their athletic shorts. Women (but not men) had a curfew—they had to be in by a certain time every night. There was a definite double standard, but no one screamed "discrimination." "We went to school in the dark ages," Ruth's friend Alice Freed recalled. In the 1950s, women just didn't complain about having to live by different standards from men. "In our day, we accepted it."[2]

Women's rights were hardly an issue in the 1950s. NOW, the National Organization for Women, did not yet exist. Controversy over ERA, the Equal Rights Amendment, was still some years away. The word *feminist* did not have the widespread usage that it would a decade later to describe a person who strongly and actively supports women's rights. "I did not think of myself as a feminist in the 1950s," Ruth said many years later. "The subject never even came up in my conversations with classmates or teachers."[3] There were, however, small signs of discontent among some college women who questioned where their long hours of study were leading them. Graffiti scratched on a college library wall said what was on the minds of Ruth and many other women students: "Study hard, get good grades, get your degree, get married, have three rotten kids, die and be buried."[4] Was there really no more to a woman's career than this?

Was she supposed to pursue a college education only to end up washing dishes and diapers? Many women of the 1950s were beginning to ask these questions—if only silently.

Despite the double standards, Ruth pursued her studies at Cornell with the same seriousness and dedication she had shown in high school. Professor Robert E. Cushman, under whom she studied constitutional law, became her mentor— her trusted teacher, adviser, and friend. Among the many valuable things Cushman taught her was how to write well, a quality she says is essential to being a good lawyer. When the professor read her papers, he would correct not only the content but her style and writing skills as well. Another professor who had a profound influence on Ruth's writing was Vladimir Nabokov. "He loved words," she recalled, "the sound of words. . . . Even when I write an opinion, I will often read a sentence aloud and [ask] 'Can I say this in fewer words—can I write it so the meaning will come across with greater clarity?'"[5]

But it was Professor Cushman, for whom Ruth worked as a research assistant, who piqued her interest in law. "He was a very gentle man," she recalled. "But he could not tolerate threats to our American way."[6] In the 1950s, one of the gravest threats to the American way came from Senator

Joseph McCarthy, who terrorized politicians and other well-known Americans by accusing them of belonging to the Communist Party. To his supporters, he was a great patriot, dedicated to keeping the United States free from communism. But to most Americans, "McCarthyism" spelled fear and suspicion. As the communist scare spread across the country, some people suspected even their closest friends of being "Red." Senator McCarthy often used unethical and illegal means to accuse his victims. His witch-hunting techniques were a great threat to democracy and the American way of life. McCarthy's tactics angered Professor Cushman, who supported justice and fairness, and he resolved to help defend people against McCarthy's attacks.

Cushman's actions were a great inspiration to young Ruth Bader. "The McCarthy era was a time when courageous lawyers were using their legal training in support of the right to think and speak freely," she recalled. "That a lawyer could do something that was personally satisfying and at the same time work to preserve the values that have made this country great was an exciting prospect for me."[7]

Still, Ruth lacked the confidence in herself to pursue a career in law. During her third year at Cornell, she wrote a letter to her cousin Jane Gevirtz in which she confided that she really would like to become a lawyer, but she had "deep doubts on whether she had sufficient aptitude for the law."[8]

Nor did her father, Nathan, encourage her desire. He was worried by Ruth's talk of studying law. It wasn't that he objected to his daughter having a career. What bothered him was whether she could support herself as a lawyer—for, he confessed, he had little money to leave her. Wouldn't teaching be a more practical path for a woman?

One man who did support Ruth's talk of law school was a fellow student at Cornell, Martin David Ginsburg. The two met during Ruth's freshman year. Martin, then a sophomore, was one of those fortunate few students to own a car, a gray Chevrolet. One night he gave a friend a ride to pick up his date, who happened to live in the dormitory room next to Ruth's. After this chance meeting, Martin and Ruth's relationship grew closer over the next three years. "They had a marvelous romance in her senior year," remembers her cousin Jane.[9] Soon it was evident to family and friends that marriage would follow.

In her senior year, Ruth was class marshal, a responsibility that put her at the head of the line in graduation ceremonies for Cornell's College of Arts and Sciences. The day was much happier than her high school graduation had been. This time, Ruth was present to receive her many awards, for she graduated "with high honors in government and distinction in all subjects."[10] In addition, she was elected to membership in two honorary societies, one of which, Phi Beta Kappa, admits only the very brightest scholars in the country.

But the grand events of June 1954 did not end with graduation. Just a few days later, Ruth Bader and Martin Ginsburg were married in a quiet ceremony at his parents' home. Ruth's relationship to her new in-laws was a close one. Forty years later, in her Rose Garden speech at the White House, she would call her mother-in-law, Evelyn, "the most supportive parent a person could have."[11]

Acquaintances all agreed that the young couple were quite a contrast. Martin was energetic, bubbly, and outgoing. Ruth was quiet and reserved, given to long pauses when she spoke and periods of silence that sometimes made strangers uncomfortable. He became a wonderful cook; she did not. Her first home-cooked meal for Martin was tuna casserole, which, he recalls, "was as close to inedible as food could be."[12]

Still, it was a wonderful marriage. Each respected the other's talents, intelligence, and drive. Not only did Martin support his wife's talk of a career in law, but Ruth encouraged him to pursue the same career. In June 1954, Martin completed his first year at Harvard Law School. But with the Korean War in progress, he soon found his studies interrupted by duty as an army officer at Fort Sill, Oklahoma, where the couple moved soon after the wedding.

Fresh from her government studies at Cornell, Ruth took a job with the Lawton, Oklahoma, Social Security office. It was here that she experienced firsthand the discrimination that existed against women in the workplace. Not long after beginning her new job, she made the "mistake" of telling her superiors that she was pregnant. Because of her condition, they decided she could not travel across the country to a training session in Baltimore, Maryland. Ruth was rewarded for her honesty by being assigned to a lower position in the Social Security office, where she received lower pay.

In the spirit of the 1950s, she accepted her new assignment without any argument. But this injustice lit a fire in her soul that would burst into flame some ten years later, during the women's movement of the 1960s and 1970s.

Chapter / Three

Taking Up Space Where a Man Could Be

During their time at Fort Sill, Ruth spent the only year of her married life in which she did not work outside the home. On July 21, 1955, their daughter, Jane, was born. But the year was not taken up entirely with baby baths and bottles. Martin was finishing his tour of army duty and Ruth—with his encouragement—was applying again to law school. She had been accepted in 1954, but Martin's army assignment had made it impossible for her to attend.

The combination of school, marriage, and motherhood looked to her like "an overwhelming burden." Indeed it was. Her father-in-law assured her that if law school and a new baby were too much to tackle together, no one would be disappointed in her. But, she remembers him saying, "if I really wanted to become a lawyer, having a baby wouldn't stand in my way. I realized he was exactly right. If you want to do something badly enough you find a way. Somehow you manage."[1]

So it was that the three Ginsburgs moved to Cambridge in 1956. Martin began his second year at Harvard Law School, and Ruth entered as a freshman, one of only nine women in a class of more than four hundred students. In those days, few women applied to law school because they feared that after graduation they might never be hired into a man's profession.

In the face of such discouraging prospects, why did Ruth Ginsburg choose law? "I became a lawyer," she says, "for personal, selfish reasons. I thought I could do a lawyer's job better than any other. I have no talent in the arts but I do write fairly well and analyze problems clearly."[2]

Martin not only encouraged his wife to study law; he made it possible for her to fit her studies into a busy schedule. From the beginning of parenthood, he shared the responsibilities. When Jane woke up in the night, it was Martin who would go to her, for he could fall back to sleep more quickly than Ruth. When Martin got home first at the end of a long day, he often cooked dinner. Without his help, Ruth admits, she might have dropped out of law school. "What Martin did went far beyond support. He believed in me more than I believed in myself."[3] A supportive husband who is willing to share duties and responsibilities is a must, she says, for any woman who hopes to combine marriage and a career.

The Ginsburgs were fortunate to find in Cambridge a grandmotherly woman who cared for Jane during the day. She arrived when Ruth left for law school in the morning and went home at 4 o'clock, when Mom returned. Martin and Ruth then juggled the evening chores to allow each of them time in the library—an essential part of any law student's day.

Although library research was of major importance, Ruth and her female colleagues soon learned that one room in Harvard's Lamont Library—the old periodicals room—was not open to women. This rule was kept as a symbol of the old days when women were not allowed in many rooms at Harvard. Late one night, finding that she absolutely had to check a reference there, Ruth pleaded with the guard to let her in. He refused; he also refused to get the magazine out of the room for her and bring it to the door. It was a small incident, but no one could deny that it was unfair. "There was no outrageous discrimination but an accumulation of small instances,"[4] Ruth recalled.

Discrimination may not have been harsh or obvious, but women law students in the 1950s clearly stood out from the men. "If you were one of two women in a section, you felt . . . that you were in plain view," Ruth explained. Women, she recalled, were more likely to be called on in the classroom than were men. "It wasn't harassment as much as it was fun and games: 'Let's call on the woman for comic relief.'"[5]

Women were simply out of place in a man's world. Judges' chambers and courtrooms had always been men's domains. Men of the 1950s found it strange, and a bit uncomfortable, to treat women as their professional equals. The point was made even clearer to the women in Ginsburg's class when Erwin Griswold, dean of the Law School, invited them to dinner at his home. How, he asked each of them, could they justify taking up space in the Law School where a man could be studying? Not knowing how to respond respectfully, Ruth mumbled that "studying law would help her better to understand her husband's work, and could possibly lead to part-time employment for herself."[6]

No one needed to worry that Ruth Ginsburg's space at Harvard Law School would be better claimed by a man. Her fellow students had the highest respect for her intelligence and dedication. One of her classmates, Ronald Loeb, later reminisced with Ruth, "While the rest of us were sulking around in dirty khaki pants and frayed button-down Oxford shirts, missing classes and complaining about all the work we had, you set a standard too high for any of us to achieve."[7]

One person who was not surprised at Ruth's tireless spirit was her husband. Throughout her first year at Harvard, while she worried about how she was doing in her classes, Martin would tell friends, with absolute faith and confidence, "My wife is going to make the *Law Review*."[8]

The *Harvard Law Review* is a scholarly journal, published by the students at Harvard Law School. It carries articles about law and court proceedings, and analyzes new laws and recent legal decisions. Legal professionals rely on the magazine to help them stay up-to-date and make important decisions. To be named to the staff of the *Harvard Law Review* is a very high honor. And, as Martin had predicted, his wife made it. Only much later did Ruth's friends confide to her that they thought Martin had lacked judgment when he had said "such a thing about a woman who didn't look particularly impressive."[9] Ruth was quick to prove them wrong.

Law Review was an honor, but it was also another responsibility to add to her growing list. Little Jane, quite mobile by now, followed her mother around the *Law Review* offices at Gannett House, crawling up and down stairs while

Mommy worked. Amazingly, Ruth didn't falter under the additional load. As Ronald Loeb later wrote, "You never missed classes; you were always prepared; your *Law Review* work was always done; you were always beautifully dressed and impeccably groomed; and you had a happy husband and a lovely young daughter."[10]

But for all her hard work at Harvard University, Ruth Ginsburg never received a degree there. In 1958, Martin graduated and took a job with a New York law firm. This meant another move for the family and a transfer of schools for Ruth. She would attend Columbia University for her final year. Although Harvard sometimes granted diplomas to students who transferred, Ruth received no such offer. Not until 1972, when she was becoming a well-known lawyer in the field of women's rights, did the law school offer her a diploma. No thanks, Ginsburg told them; the recognition had come too late.

Meanwhile, the class of 1959 at Columbia University Law School was worried about rumors of the Ginsburgs' move to New York. "We had heard that the smartest person on the East Coast was going to transfer, and that we were all going to drop down one rank,"[11] said Nina Appel, now dean of a Chicago law school. The Columbia students had good reason to worry about their rank in class.

Soon after her transfer, Ruth was named to the *Columbia Law Review*, a magazine as well respected as the Harvard publication. And by the end of her year at Columbia—her final year of law school—Ruth Ginsburg was tied for first in her class. "When you met Ruth, you knew that she was very serious and smart and did things with a minimum of fuss,"[12] said a Columbia student, now a justice on the New Jersey Supreme Court.

Just as in her senior year at Cornell, and earlier at James Madison High, graduation day brought many awards and honors. But this time there was a surprise during the ceremonies. As Ruth Ginsburg walked down the aisle to receive her diploma, Jane's young voice announced loudly and clearly to the hundreds of people in the audience, "That's my Mommy!"[13]

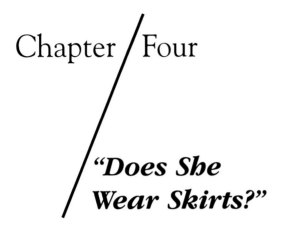

Chapter /Four

"Does She Wear Skirts?"

Phi Beta Kappa, *Harvard* and *Columbia Law Reviews*, first in her class . . . And yet, following her graduation from Columbia, "Not a single law firm in the entire city of New York bid for my employment."[1] Even the law office where Ginsburg had worked during the summer—and had done an excellent job—did not offer to hire her. Why not? What was wrong?

There were a number of reasons. "In the fifties, the traditional law firms were just beginning to turn around on hiring Jews. . . . They had just gotten over that form of discrimination. But to be a woman, a Jew, and a mother to boot, that combination was a bit much."[2] Very likely, motherhood was the biggest obstacle, says Ruth. Employers worried that she wouldn't be able to give full time and attention to her work. In 1959, Americans believed the "perfect mother" stayed at home to raise her children. The devoted mother and housewife was the "crown princess,"[3] recalled Ruth. A working mother just didn't fit into this picture.

But Ruth Ginsburg was not a person to accept rejection. When she had no employment offers, recalled a longtime friend and judge, "steel entered her soul."[4] She simply refused to take no for an answer. She would not believe that she could not compete in a man's world.

At long last, she got a break. A Harvard Law School professor called to say he would like to recommend her for a position as clerk in the office of Felix Frankfurter, a justice on the United States Supreme Court. Clerking for a Supreme Court justice was a highly coveted position for students just out of law school. Ruth's academic record, along with a strong recommendation from the professor, made her a very likely choice. Hearing that she had been recommended, Justice Frankfurter asked one of his associates, "Does she wear skirts? I can't stand girls in pants!"[5] Certainly, he was assured, Ruth wore skirts. Nevertheless, Justice Frankfurter didn't call Ginsburg for an interview. He turned her down "simply because he wasn't ready to hire a woman."[6]

Fortunately there *was* a man in the legal profession who was willing to take a chance on a woman. That was Edmund L. Palmieri, a U.S. District Court judge for the Southern District of New York, who hired Ginsburg as a clerk in his office. Determined to prove that she could do an outstanding job, despite being a wife and mother, Ruth put all her energy into her new position. "I worked harder than any other law clerk in the building, stayed late whenever it was necessary, sometimes when it wasn't necessary, came in Saturdays, and brought work home."[7] Judge Palmieri appreciated Ruth's dedication to the job, and the two became good friends.

But the sting of being a woman in a man's profession continued to haunt her. One of the many people who had turned her down for a job was the famous Learned Hand. Hand was an influential judge who served in the federal courts longer than any other person. Although he was never on the Supreme Court, he is said to have had a greater mind than many of its justices. Judge Palmieri drove Hand to and from work, and often Ruth rode in the backseat. One day Judge Hand explained why he had not hired her. It was because he sometimes used off-color language that might be offensive to a lady; he had "too salty a tongue," he confessed. Quickly Ruth pointed out to him that he made no effort to curb his language while they were in the car. What was the difference, she wanted to know? "Young lady," he told her, "here [in the car] I am not looking you in the face."[8]

For two years, Ruth Ginsburg clerked for Judge Palmieri. She found the work very stimulating, and a warm relationship grew between them. She calls him "a man I deeply admired, whose friendship I cherished to this day."[9] When the clerkship ended, in 1961, Ruth found her job prospects greatly improved.

By now she had become very interested in writing, doing legal research, and teaching law. After much hard thought, she turned down an attractive offer from a New York law firm and chose instead to join Professor Hans Smit in Columbia Law School's Project on International Procedure.

Ginsburg's part in the project was to study Sweden's judicial system and the way it processed legal matters. As part of her work, she learned the Swedish language and spent a total of six months living in that country. "Going off to a foreign land I knew nothing about and being wholly on my own" were two of the reasons she says she took the position. Another was the chance to write a book. "The idea that I would have something of my own between hard covers was tremendously appealing."[10]

During the first year, while she was a research associate on the project, Ruth traveled to the city of Lund, Sweden. Jane, a first-grader, went over to meet her mother when school was out, and Martin joined them during his vacation. "My 'professional association' with my mother began at a very early age,"[11] Jane jokes. While her mother worked, Jane spent time at the University of Lund's day-care center for children of students and staff.

The next year, Ruth waited until school was out to leave for Sweden, so Jane could travel with her. This time, they headed to Stockholm, where Ginsburg served as associate director for the Project on International Procedure. Jane spent that summer at a children's home, like a summer camp, in a rural area south of the city. Studying in Sweden opened Ruth's eyes to the progress that Swedish women had made in the workforce. It was these observations, she said, that "first stirred feminist feelings"[12] in her.

Her research on the project completed, Ruth returned home in 1963 to finish writing her book about Swedish law, which was published two years later. Again young Jane was involved professionally with her mother. She helped her to proofread the text—although she was not yet ten years old!

By the end of the international project, Ginsburg had decided she wanted to teach law. At Rutgers University Law School in New Jersey, a black professor was leaving his job as instructor

Ruth with her daughter, Jane, in 1965

of civil procedure, a course that taught students the proper methods of handling legal cases. Ginsburg was hired to fill the position. To her delight, she discovered that the school already had a woman on its staff; this was obviously a progressive university, one that gave opportunities to minorities and women, and she was excited to be part of it.

Throughout her time as a teacher at Rutgers, the Ginsburgs continued to share family duties. Martin did much of his work at home and kept an office close to the house. Having two working parents made Jane independent at an early age. It was up to her to get to school on time—a private school in New York where, she confesses, she had a "mixed" record. In the early years, "I didn't have many friends, and my behavior was very bad."[13] Often her teachers had negative reports for Ruth and Martin about their daughter's conduct.

Still, Jane says, she never resented having a working mother. "I think I rather enjoyed my situation. Since I was alone so much, I had more freedom. I got away with a lot." Like buying and eating candy after school (a strict no-no) and then lying to cover up her act. With lawyers for parents, however, the child stood little chance of a light sentence. "My parents were not permissive,"[14] says Jane. They generally agreed on discipline, but Dad was the one most likely to carry out the punishment.

For nine years, Ruth remained at Rutgers. "I found I liked teaching. I liked the sense of being my own boss." Unlike working for a law firm, where lawyers must devote themselves entirely to their clients' needs, Ruth discovered that teaching gave her a great deal of flexibility. "There's tremendous luxury in being a law teacher in that you can spend most of your time doing whatever interests you."[15]

It was while she was teaching at Rutgers that Ginsburg's interest in sex discrimination law was born. Her students were the ones who planted the seed in her mind. At that time, discrimination complaints from women were coming into the New Jersey office of the American Civil Liberties Union. The ACLU, an organization formed in 1920 to protect human rights, was just beginning to hear from women who felt their rights were being denied. Their cases were referred to her, Ginsburg says, "because, well, sex discrimination was regarded as a woman's job. . . . Both the ACLU and my students prodded me to take an active part in the effort to eliminate senseless gender lines in the law." The more seriously she considered the idea, the more she realized how much this type of legal work appealed to her. She began to have "high hopes for significant change in the next decade."[16]

But along with the new focus in her career came a new focus at home. On September 8, 1965, the Ginsburgs' son, James Steven, was born.

Juggling a career and family life had never been easy, but now it was next to impossible. At the same time, Ruth's father, Nathan, became very ill and moved in with the family, adding to her responsibilities. Still, she never considered leaving her teaching job.

Jane was a big help to her working parents. Ten years old when her brother was born, she made a good baby-sitter on Sunday mornings when they wanted to sleep. She didn't mind it, she says, because it allowed her to skip Sunday school at the synagogue. "I also used my chores as an excuse to get out of a lot of other things I didn't want to do."[17]

Did Ruth ever feel that she was not giving enough time to her children and husband? Did she feel guilty about dividing her life between a career and her family? Occasionally, yes. One of those times was the day young James put Drāno crystals in his mouth. The housekeeper who had been caring for him rushed him to the hospital, but when Ruth and Martin arrived, they were stunned. The strong chemical drain cleaner had distorted James's face with deep burns. "Charred lips encircled his mouth—a tiny, burnt-out cavern, ravaged by the lye."[18] Fortunately, the child was left with barely a scar, but his mother suffered tremendous guilt. It wasn't that she blamed the housekeeper or

James as a little boy. In later years, he would say that his mother was "always there when I wanted her to be— and even when I didn't."

felt that the accident wouldn't have happened had she been there. She blamed herself for having left the poison within the child's reach. Like so many working parents, Ruth was discovering that it was often a painful tug-of-war to be both a dedicated homemaker and a prized professional.

Ruth the feminist—at work for the Women's Rights Project

Chapter /Five

The Women's Rights Project

At the dawn of the 1960s, the women's movement in America had made little progress. But by the end of that decade, women were campaigning in the streets, on college campuses, and in the courts for equal treatment under the law. President John F. Kennedy provided momentum in 1961 by creating the Commission on the Status of Women. After studying the commission's work, Congress passed the Equal Pay Act two years later. This act required that working women receive the same pay as men for doing the same type of work. It was the first federal law concerning women's rights to be passed since 1920, when women were granted the right to vote.

The Feminine Mystique, a book by Betty Friedan published in 1963, brought the women's movement alive. Millions of women across the country began to believe that they could do more with their lives than care for children and cook meals. "As she made the beds, shopped for groceries, matched slip-cover material, ate peanut butter sandwiches with her children, chauffeured Cub Scouts and Brownies, lay beside her husband at night—she was afraid to ask even of herself the silent question—'Is this all?'"[1] So begins Friedan's book, the launchpad from which the feminist movement soared. Three years later, Friedan helped to found NOW, the National Organization for Women, a group that fought to ensure equality for women in education, employment, politics, and the courts.

It was not so much Friedan's writing, however, as author Simone de Beauvoir's *The Second Sex*, that inspired Ginsburg's interest in the feminist movement. She responded by immersing herself in a study of women's law. But soon she discovered that there was little to study; women's issues simply had not been brought before the courts. "My consciousness was awakened," she recalls. She began to question how women had been putting up with unfair treatment and practices. "How have I been putting up with them?"[2] she wondered.

Throughout the 1960s and 1970s, America moved toward greater equality of the sexes. The 1964 Civil Rights Act made it illegal to discriminate against someone because of race or gender

(sex). No longer could women be treated differently from men in issues of voting, education, employment, or access to public places. This act was followed, in 1967, by President Lyndon Johnson's
executive order that forbade sex discrimination by
any government agency or companies holding government contracts.

The problem now became enforcement of
these orders. It was one thing for Congress or the
states to pass nondiscrimination acts. But it was
something else to see that the new rules actually
were followed. Quietly, methodically, in her professional, businesslike way, Ruth Bader Ginsburg set
out to ensure that women actually received the
equal treatment they were promised. "Ruthless
Ruthie,"[3] her classmates at Harvard had called
her, because once she committed to a project, she
worked tirelessly at it, never stopping until she
had reached her goal. Now Ruthless Ruthie applied
that same determination to the problem of gender
discrimination.

Ginsburg's new link with the ACLU was, she
decided, the perfect platform on which to build a
legal foundation for women's rights. The first big
test case came in 1970. *Reed v.* (against) *Reed*
involved a law in the state of Idaho that gave preference to men over women in handling the estates
of deceased relatives or friends. The Idaho law

seemed to violate the Fourteenth Amendment to the U.S. Constitution, which said that no state shall "deny to any person . . . the equal protection of the laws."[4]

Ginsburg led the ACLU's attack to strike down the Idaho law. After lower courts had heard the case, the battle of *Reed v. Reed* was finally fought in the United States Supreme Court. The High Court justices decided that the Idaho law *was* unconstitutional; it *did* violate the Fourteenth Amendment. "It was the first time," recalled Ginsburg, that "the Supreme Court ever overturned a law in response to a woman's complaint of unfair sex-based discrimination."[5] Although Ginsburg herself did not argue the case in court, she was the main author of the brief—the written explanation of the case's major points and arguments. Her work became known as the "grandmother brief," for it was the ancestor of many future legal opinions on women's rights.

Winning *Reed v. Reed* was a major step forward for the women's movement in the courts. So delighted was the ACLU by the Supreme Court's decision that it voted to set up a special department, the Women's Rights Project, to deal with women's issues. The project's goal was to explain to judges, lawyers, employers, and other professional people the meaning of "sex stereotyping"—the thoughtless and unfair grouping of all men into one category and all women into another. Decision makers needed to understand, Ginsburg said, "how the notion that men are this way (frogs, snails, puppy dogs' tails) and women are that way (sugar, spice, everything nice) ends up hurting both sexes."[6]

After the success of *Reed v. Reed*, Ginsburg was made a codirector of the Women's Rights Project, a move that the *Columbia Law Review* said did much to increase the organization's respectability. At the same time, she ended her nine-year career at Rutgers and accepted a tenured teaching position at Columbia Law School. Tenure is offered only to respected professionals. It ensures that a person will not be dismissed from the job except for severe misconduct, and then only after a formal hearing. Ruth Ginsburg was the first woman to achieve this rank at Columbia. At the start of her new position, she agreed to devote half her hours to the Women's Rights Project. Ginsburg handled litigation— researching and arguing cases in court for the WRP. Her codirector, Brenda Feigen Fasteau, managed the project's day-to-day operations.

By the early 1970s, so many sex discrimination cases were being brought before the courts that the numbers threatened "to obstruct . . . equal rights for women."[7] It was hard for the courts to know

Ruth Ginsburg during her time as a professor of law at Columbia University

which ones they should choose to hear. WRP leaders decided to handle only those cases that they thought would be solid stepping-stones on the road to women's equality. They chose cases concerning employment because the idea of "equal pay for equal work" was now seen as fair by most Americans. Employment cases, Ginsburg believed, would be more apt to win in the courts.

The WRP rejected cases that it considered frivolous or silly. "We tried to figure out," said Ruth, "the issues that were ripe for change through litigation and the ones that were likely to fail."[8] The WRP wanted to win its cases, not only because it sought to build its reputation but because each win strengthened the position of women's rights in the courts.

And yet it wasn't strictly *women's* rights that concerned Ruth Ginsburg and the WRP. The broader issue was *gender* rights—equal treatment for both sexes. Ginsburg's goal was to show that "laws that discriminated between men and women—even those laws that were meant to help women—were based on unfair and even harmful stereotypes and were in most cases unconstitutional."[9] The WRP wanted to "get rid of these gender labels in the law."[10]

A great opportunity arose in the case of *Frontiero v. Richardson.* The plaintiffs (the people filing the suit) were Sharon Frontiero, a lieutenant in the air force, and her husband, Joseph. They challenged a law that made it easier for women to be claimed as dependents by their husbands than for men to be claimed by their wives. A woman could be called dependent even if she did not depend on her husband's income. But a man had to show that more than half of his financial support came from his wife in order for him to be called a dependent. Although the law appeared to give women preference over men, Ginsburg believed that unequal treatment in any form was harmful to the status of women. She argued that "women were branded inferior through such treatment."[11]

The case went to the United States Supreme Court, where Ruth Ginsburg argued in favor of gender equality. It was her first appearance before America's highest court, and, she admitted, "I was terribly nervous. In fact, I didn't eat lunch for fear that I might throw up." But as she stood before the nine justices, "I felt a surge of power that carried me through."[12] In presenting her argument, she quoted nineteenth-century feminist Sarah Grimké, saying, "I ask no favor for my sex. All I ask of our brethren [brothers] is that they take their feet off our necks. . . . Thank you."[13] Ginsburg won the case, the justices voting 8 to 1 in favor of her argument. The rules that defined a dependent were now the same for men as for women. It was a giant step forward for the WRP.

The *Frontiero* victory came on the heels of another major case in the women's movement—the 1973 decision on abortion in *Roe v. Wade*. Ruth Ginsburg and the WRP were not involved in arguing this case, but it did have a major impact on the women's movement. *Roe v. Wade* challenged a Texas law that prohibited a woman from having an abortion, and the case went to the Supreme Court. Here the justices decided, 7 to 2, that states could not stop a woman from having an abortion during the first three months of pregnancy. To do so would violate her right to privacy, the right to decide for herself what she would do. But during the second trimester (three-month period) of pregnancy, when the unborn baby might have a chance of living outside the mother's body, the states could, under certain conditions, have a voice in the abortion decision.

Feminists called *Roe v. Wade* a great step forward for women's rights, but Ruth Ginsburg did not completely agree. First, she felt that the case should have emphasized the equal standing of women in our society, along with the right to privacy, which became the major issue. Second, she believed that instead of setting up strict rules for the states to follow about abortion, the Court should simply have overturned the Texas law and left it at that. "Suppose the court had stopped there," she suggested. That move might have "served to reduce rather than to fuel controversy."[14]

Ginsburg wished that the justices had moved slower on the abortion issue, building a step-by-step foundation in the courts. She would have preferred to let each state decide for itself how to handle abortion rights, as long as the rules they set did not violate the U.S. Constitution. Ginsburg felt that *Roe* "halted a political process that was moving in a reform direction," and that it "prolonged divisiveness"[15] and caused bitter arguments between the two sides. In many ways she was right. Over the years, the *Roe v. Wade* decision has muddied the abortion issue and confused the courts. This confusion has helped to strengthen the stand of the antiabortion, or right to life, movement.

Roe's main point, however, is one with which Ruth Ginsburg agrees. The decision recognizes reproductive choice as a human right, which strengthens Ginsburg's stand on equal citizenship for men and women. In her methodical way—the way she wished the Supreme Court had moved on *Roe*—she continued to build a firm legal foundation for the Women's Rights Project. Over the next three years, the WRP handled more than thirty cases involving gender rights, which brought

Ginsburg before the Supreme Court several more times. Her style was quiet, professional, businesslike—and highly effective. Those who heard her in court said the nine justices would "sit up straight when she spoke." With each appearance, they "grew even more respectful, and ruled in her favor five of the six times she argued."[16]

Despite her successes, Ginsburg was never as comfortable expressing herself orally as she was in writing. To be effective in speaking before the Court, she had to rely on an inner strength and confidence that have helped her survive many tough personal appearances. What gives her this strength? Often, she says, she thinks of her mother when she is in situations that demand a perfect performance. "When I argue before the . . . Court, I wear her earrings and her pin and I think how pleased she would be if she were there."[17]

Although she is a strong supporter of women's rights, Ginsburg often represented men. Taking on men's cases helped to prove that her goal was not simply women's rights but the right of all people to be treated equally under the law, without regard to gender. In the case of *Craig v. Boren,* she represented a man who claimed discrimination under an Oklahoma law that allowed women to buy low-alcohol beer at age eighteen, while men had to be twenty-one. It was a clear case of sex discrimina-

Celia Bader, Ruth's mother. Although she died while Ruth was in high school, she remained a strong influence on her daughter throughout her life.

tion, and the Supreme Court agreed with Ginsburg's claims. *Craig v. Boren* was one of those cases
that stood a strong chance of winning from the
beginning. Its victory placed another brick in the
firm foundation of the WRP.

Still, the sailing was not entirely smooth, as
Ruth would learn in *Kahn v. Shevin*. This case
involved a Florida law that allowed widows (but
not widowers) to take a $15 deduction on property
tax. Even though the deduction was small, why
should one sex be given preference over another?
the WRP wanted to know. Once again, Ruth
Ginsburg found herself arguing *against* a law that
gave women an advantage over men. But this time,
the High Court's decision was not so favorable to
Ruth. Justice William O. Douglas, who had a history of supporting women's rights, now voted to
uphold the Florida law. His decision surprised
Ginsburg tremendously. Only later, when she read
his autobiography, *Go East*, did she learn about the
hardships his mother had faced as a widow, when
Douglas himself was just five years old. This, she
decided, must have been the reason for his vote in
Kahn v. Shevin. It was the only Supreme Court case
that Ruth Ginsburg lost during her time with the
Women's Rights Project.

The *Kahn* setback did little to stop the progress
of the WRP. Soon Ginsburg was in court again, rep-

resenting a young New Jersey man's claims to his wife's Social Security benefits. Stephen Wiesenfeld was left with the care of his infant son when his wife, Paula, died in childbirth. The government assumed that because he was a man, Stephen had been the primary wage earner in his family, and that Paula's income was only an "extra." But the truth was that Paula's income had been almost twice that of Stephen's. He wrote to Ginsburg, telling her that he needed his wife's Social Security checks in order to raise his son. If he were a widow, he pointed out, he could receive them without question. But because he was a man, the rules made it difficult or impossible for him to claim his wife's benefits.

It was a case tailor-made for Ruth Bader Ginsburg. This was exactly the kind of sex stereotyping the WRP was fighting to eliminate. Why should men and women be treated differently simply because of their gender? This case, said Ginsburg, "hammered down the point that the court just could not get away with saying, 'Well, this is all right because it compensates women.'"[18] The law had to be fair, and to give one sex preference over another was not fair. Ultimately Stephen Wiesenfeld's case got to the U.S. Supreme Court, where the justices decided that Social Security benefits could not be paid differently just because of gender. Wiesenfeld won his case, and Ruth Ginsburg won another victory for the WRP.

But in spite of her victories, the fight to ensure equal treatment for both sexes was not completely won. October 1976 found Ginsburg back before the Supreme Court, again defending a man's claim to his widow's Social Security benefits. In Washington to hear Ruth argue the case was her daughter, Jane, by now a budding law student herself. The government claimed that plaintiff Goldfarb was not entitled to his widow's Social Security benefits because her wages had amounted to less than half the family's income. But this same standard did not apply to a widow who was collecting her deceased husband's benefits; widows were allowed to receive the payments.

When the Goldfarb case was heard by a lower court, Ginsburg recalls, the judge said, "I don't like this, but I don't have any choice after *Frontiero* and *Wiesenfeld*."[19] It was exciting for Ruth to hear that the decisions in the WRP's earlier cases were helping to strengthen the Goldfarb case. At the Supreme Court, the justices agreed that the government's policy *did* discriminate against Goldfarb, because it set different standards for paying benefits to men than to women. It was another victory for gender rights.

Ruth Bader Ginsburg was perhaps the major

Visiting daughter Jane, herself a student at Harvard Law School, in 1978

reason that the WRP was successful in winning these landmark cases. "She is," says Kathleen Peratis, a former attorney with the ACLU, "just the most spectacular lawyer I have ever met." She calls Ginsburg "very exacting" and "critical" but very fair. "Always she is most appreciative of superior effort."[20]

In the courtroom, Ruth Ginsburg is quiet and reserved, but she makes her arguments firmly and convincingly. She is a master at getting her listeners—whether students or Supreme Court justices—to understand her points. Even when speaking to the most sophisticated judges in the country, she uses clear, precise language and offers examples to make herself understood. As she told the High Court in a 1975 sex discrimination case, "Laws of this quality help to keep women, not on a pedestal, but in a cage." Another time, she reminded justices that the law "must deal with the parent, not the mother; with the homemaker, not the housewife; and with the surviving spouse, not the widow."[21]

Ginsburg speaks slowly and with caution, as if she is picking each word especially for this moment, this particular sentence. Sometimes people are uncomfortable with her long pauses, but it does make them attentive listeners. When arguing a case, she rarely gets emotional; an air of calmness surrounds her. She is self-assured but not cocky,

Spending time with the family—husband Martin, son James, and daughter Jane

drawing on her vast education and knowledge of the law to support her points.

Ruth Ginsburg's career with the WRP was highly demanding and required long hours of legal study and preparation. During her eight years of service as legal counsel to the Women's Rights Project, she also taught constitutional law and civil procedure at Columbia University. And yet, stresses her son, James, she was still able to be an excellent mother. "The family was always home for dinner. . . . A night did not go by when my mother did not check to see that I was doing my schoolwork. She was always there when I wanted her to be—and even when I didn't."[22]

Chapter / Six

The United States Court of Appeals

Is she "aloof or simply shy?" the *New York Times* wondered. Is she "steely or just cold?"[1] Ruth Ginsburg's lifelong friends say there is no question about the softness of her heart, but they admit that it can be difficult to make her smile. Even Jane, as a small child, recognized her mother's seriousness, and kept track of those rare days in a little book she called *Mommy Laughs*.

Although people may have trouble understanding some sides of Ruth Ginsburg's personality, no one questions her tireless devotion to her work. She allows no wasted moments. While she was teaching, she would read her mail on the subway and make her final plans for class on the train. Her husband, Martin, confesses that "she often works in cabs on the way to the theater." Rest is not a big part of her schedule; many nights she gets just three or four hours of sleep. During these long, late-night work sessions, her favorite companions are coffee and bunches of grapes. "I guess I work this way," says Ruth, "because I am so fussy about the quality of the product."[2]

That concern with quality doesn't always win her praise, however. Ginsburg's critics call her "picky, demanding, academic and school-marmish."[3] But even they cannot deny her superb intelligence and knowledge of the law. She is a woman of principle, basing every decision on a proper code of conduct and a set of solid beliefs. In fact, says a fellow Washington lawyer, "she's so principled, she's unpredictable."[4] She may offer an opinion that seems to contradict her personal feelings, just because of principle. That was the case in *Roe v. Wade*, when Ginsburg criticized the Supreme Court's reasoning. Although she supported a woman's right to an abortion, she felt that the principle in this case should have been equal rights for women as well as the right to privacy.

Ruth Ginsburg's strong principles allow her to see the rightness and fairness of an issue, even when it conflicts with her personal feelings. This quality is crucial in a good judge, who is expected to issue unbiased decisions. And it was this very quality for which President Jimmy Carter was searching when he looked for a new judge to serve on the United States Court of Appeals in 1980. Not surprisingly, he found it in Ruth Bader Ginsburg, whom he nominated for the court's District of Columbia Circuit. After her excellent record with the WRP, Ginsburg's nomination was quickly approved, and she took the oath of office on June 30, 1980.

The United States Court of Appeals is considered by some to be the second highest court in the nation, just below the Supreme Court in the scope of its power and rulings. Each state is assigned to one of eleven "circuits," or regions in the country. The District of Columbia makes up the twelfth circuit, and it was to this one that Ginsburg was appointed to serve with ten other judges. Cases usually come to the federal appeals courts from one of the eighty-nine district courts across the United States. When the losing party in a case feels that it did not receive a fair trial in district court, it may ask an appeals court, the next higher level above the district courts, to reconsider the case and possibly issue a new decision. In appeals court, the case is not retried before a jury—the group of people selected to hear evidence and statements from witnesses in a trial. Instead, lawyers prepare briefs for the judges to read. A panel of three of the judges must read the

In the robes of appellate court judge, 1980

briefs and hear the lawyers' arguments in the case. Based on the facts, the judges may affirm (agree with) or reverse (change) the decision of the district court.

The U.S. district courts and appeals courts, as well as the Supreme Court, are all *federal* courts; they usually hear cases that involve federal (nationwide) laws or the United States Constitution. The appeals court system was set up to relieve the load on the Supreme Court, which was having a record number of cases brought before it. Appeals court judges must base their rulings on previous decisions made by the Supreme Court in related cases. They must interpret federal laws and uphold the Constitution and its amendments.

Ginsburg warns, however, that a strict interpretation of the Constitution is unworkable today. For example, she points out, when the Constitution was written two centuries ago, the only voters were white, male property owners. Since then, this and many other aspects of our society have changed greatly. Still, Americans cherish this document, Ginsburg stresses, because as our society evolves, we can adapt the Constitution — either by amendments or by judges' decisions — to use as a guide at any point in our history.

Being a judge, with the responsibility of interpreting federal laws and the Constitution, represented a major change in the direction of Ruth Ginsburg's life. For nearly a decade, she had been an advocate—a person who stood strongly in favor of an issue or a cause. In Ginsburg's case, the issue was gender rights. Now, as a judge, she would have to separate her personal feelings from the facts and principles of each case. She felt that she could not remain an advocate and be a good judge at the same time. "One of the most sacred duties of a judge," she said, referring to a speech by former Supreme Court Justice Oliver Wendell Holmes, "is not to read her convictions [personal beliefs] into the Constitution."[5] Her own desires, she felt, had no place on a judge's bench.

In the years ahead, Ruth Bader Ginsburg would be compared with Thurgood Marshall, who, as a lawyer, had been a strong civil rights advocate. Even after he was appointed the first black justice on the U.S. Supreme Court, Marshall continued to speak out in support of civil rights, and his decisions as a judge often reflected his personal feelings. "Unlike Thurgood Marshall," said one civil rights lawyer recently, "Ruth stopped being an advocate when she went on the court."[6]

Throughout her career as an appeals court judge, Ginsburg relied on principle to help her make fair decisions. "On the bench," wrote one reporter, she showed "little of the passion that so fueled her earlier work"[7] (with the Women's Rights Project). Rather than ruling as her heart might have wanted, Judge Ginsburg showed herself to be "a cautious and fine-grained jurist, respectful of precedent."[8]

Precedent—decisions made in the past by other courts and judges that have shaped the framework of American law—was a principle on which Ginsburg relied heavily in deciding cases. When she disagreed with fellow appeals court judges, or found a case in conflict with her own opinions, she let precedent guide her. How had similar cases been decided in the past? To get the answers, Ginsburg (like all good judges) researched the history of every related case to see how earlier judges had ruled and what principles had guided them.

So strongly did precedent and principle shape Ruth Ginsburg's decisions that it was hard to predict how she would vote on certain issues. When she joined the appeals court in 1980, she was a well-known liberal. She favored change and progress in society, as shown in her work for women's rights. Most appeals court judges who are appointed by a Democratic president (as was Ginsburg) tend to vote in a liberal way. Because she was a liberal, people expected her to vote with other liberal judges on the court. They did not imagine that she could agree with the conservatives, who tend to be less in favor of change and reform.

Yet she often surprised people by voting with the more conservative members of the court. Soon it became clear that Ruth Ginsburg could not be termed either a liberal or a conservative. She was a centrist—in the center of the political scale—independent of either the liberal left or the conservative right. Ginsburg decided each case individually, basing her decisions on precedent, principle, and the facts put before her. Court watchers found it very difficult to predict how she would vote on future issues.

In the 1984 case of *Goldman v. Secretary of Defense*, for example, Ginsburg supported the right of a Jewish military officer to wear a yarmulke, a religious head covering, when he was on duty. To deny people this right, she said, goes against "the best of our traditions" to "accommodate the public service to [people's] spiritual needs."[9] Her opinion was dissenting, which meant that she disagreed with the majority of the judges on the case.

In another case, she supported a law to let private attorneys investigate claims of wrongdoing by high-level government officials. Such a law, she said, did not violate the U.S. Constitution's guidelines as to how misconduct by government officials should be handled.

In 1992 she voted against a Washington, D.C., program that set aside contracts for companies owned by members of minority groups. In explaining her decision, she claimed that the plan did not follow an earlier Supreme Court ruling. That ruling stated that before officials could set aside contracts for minorities, they must prove that discrimination really did exist; minorities should not be awarded the contracts automatically.

During her years on the appeals court, Judge Ginsburg showed that she simply could not be second-guessed; she considered each case individually, relying on precedent and principle. In fact, *Legal Times* magazine reported in 1988 that Ruth Ginsburg sided more often with conservative judges on the appeals court than with liberal judges.

Her unpredictable stand had advantages for the court, however. During her thirteen years as an appeals court judge, she became "a bridge builder on the . . . divided appeals court." When the judges disagreed on an issue, when they could not come to a consensus, or majority opinion, Ruth Ginsburg often brought them together. She was a master at helping each side understand the views of the other. Said Washington lawyer Peter Huber, who once clerked for Ginsburg, she "knows how to

disagree without being disagreeable and has mas-
tered the art so well she pulls people her way."[10] It
was this reputation as a consensus builder—her
ability to get two opposing sides to agree on an
issue—that would one day bring Ruth Bader
Ginsburg into the national judicial spotlight.

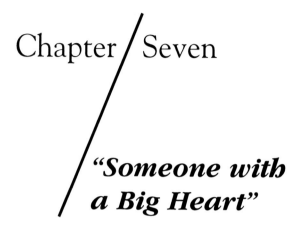

Chapter / Seven

"Someone with a Big Heart"

During Ruth Ginsburg's term as an appeals court judge, Columbia University Law School decided to pay her an honor. Amid much ceremony, the school unveiled a portrait of its former professor that it planned to hang beside those of famous Supreme Court justices like Charles Evans Hughes and Harlan Fiske Stone. This would be the first time a woman's portrait had ever hung in the gallery of greats at Columbia.

There was just one problem. Ginsburg did not recognize herself in the painting. It pictured her as a very large, physically imposing person. Today the portrait does not hang in the hall at Columbia; it is locked in storage, out of sight.

The image that often characterizes Ginsburg is a serious one. One report calls her "shy to the point of discomfort,"[1] a trait that may paint an unfair picture of her as a cold, standoffish person. Physical appearance may also contribute to this image. Her straight brown hair is pulled back tight against her head and tied with a ribbon in what one reporter calls "her trademark bun."[2] Dark, serious eyes stare out at you from above a firm, tight-set mouth. Her quietness sometimes makes people feel uncomfortable. A friend who was at a dinner party with her recalls that Ruth didn't speak most of the night, acting "as if there were a wall around her."[3] And yet others, who work with her every day, call Ruth Ginsburg very gracious, warm, and sociable. They say she is a charmer, extremely attentive and thoughtful of others.

Perhaps her firm manner in the courtroom makes her appear more forbidding than she really is. One report in the *Almanac of the Federal Judiciary* called her "sarcastic" and "intimidating," yet another said, "I've never seen her raise her voice. She's absolutely the most polite judge."[4] Ginsburg follows her own advice that "an effective judge [should] speak in 'a moderate and restrained' voice."[5] Her words come out slowly, almost haltingly, often causing tension among her listeners, "the tension perhaps of a brain ticking,"[6] says one acquaintance. The content of her speech is also "moderate and restrained." Ginsburg does not take a radical stand on most issues nor state her opin-

ions in a loud, demanding way. She thinks through every detail of a decision in a painstaking, methodical manner.

Nevertheless, when President Bill Clinton first met Ruth Bader Ginsburg, he found himself "charmed by her humility," her humbleness, and not "put off by her lack of assertiveness."[7] He liked her modest, quiet manner. Like certain other observers, Clinton was able to see through her cool, imposing appearance into the warmth of her heart.

Ginsburg first came to the president's attention in 1993, when he was looking for a Supreme Court justice to replace the retiring Byron White. At the beginning of his search, he announced that he was seeking a person with "a fine mind, good judgment, wide experience in the law and the problems of real people, and someone with a big heart."[8]

It was extremely important for the new president to make the right choice for Supreme Court justice. Some of his nominations to fill other top government posts had brought him severe criticism. When reporters and senators looked into the backgrounds of these people, they found wrongdoing that caused embarrassment to the White House. Clinton said this time he was looking for a Supreme Court nominee who would make people "stand up and say, 'Wow.'" He told his staff

The serious image that often characterizes Ruth Ginsburg

that with this nomination, he wanted "to hit a 'home run.'"[9]

The president's three-month search for a justice was one of the longest in U.S. history. Among the forty people Clinton considered for the position were New York Governor Mario Cuomo and Education Secretary Dick Riley. Both of them said no; commitments would not allow them to leave their current positions. More likely candidates were Interior Secretary Bruce Babbitt or Stephen G. Breyer, another appeals court judge, from the First Circuit Court in Boston. Each of these men expected to be nominated for the position; Ruth Ginsburg's name still had not been mentioned.

Clinton took his time, for he knew how important his selection would be. Supreme Court justices have tremendous influence. The eight associate justices and one chief justice on the nation's highest court are appointed for life; they serve until they die or retire. It is the justices' responsibility to interpret and explain the nation's laws and the meaning of the U.S. Constitution.

Most cases come to the Supreme Court from the federal appeals courts, like the ones on which Ginsburg and Stephen Breyer served. The losing party in an appeals court case may request a writ of certiorari, a paper asking the lower court to send up its records for review by the Supreme Court. Of the more than 6,500 cases that are brought before the High Court each term, the justices must decide which 120 or so they actually will hear. There is no time to hear more cases, since the term is short; it begins on the first Monday of October and runs until late June.

Through the years, the Supreme Court has decided cases that have had a major impact on American history. In 1857, just before the Civil War broke out, a black slave, Dred Scott, sued for his freedom when his owner took him from the slave state of Missouri into the Free State of Illinois, and then back to Missouri. The Supreme Court decided, in *Dred Scott v. Sanford*, that Scott had never ceased to be a slave and that he was not a citizen with a right to sue in court. The government had no right to take away citizens' property, the Court ruled, even if that "property" was a slave. The decision was a major setback for the rights of blacks, but it reflected the thinking in America during those times.

In 1954, the now famous case of *Brown v. Board of Education of Topeka* came before the Court. The justices agreed that the idea of "separate but equal" schools for blacks and whites violated the equal protection clause of the Fourteenth Amendment to the Constitution. Schools must be integrated, the Court ruled. There cannot be separate schools for separate racial groups. The lawyer representing Linda Brown in her case against the Topeka, Kansas, schools was Thurgood Marshall, who would later become the Supreme Court's first black justice.

The Court made another far-reaching decision in a 1966 case, *Miranda v. Arizona.* The justices ruled, 5 to 4, that police must inform suspects that anything they say may be used against them in court. The police must also advise suspects of their rights at the time they are arrested. Among those are the right to remain silent and the right to have an attorney present. If a police officer fails to read a suspect his or her rights, the case can be thrown out of court.

By another close vote, the Supreme Court in 1990 overturned a law passed by Congress that involved the burning of the American flag. In 1989, lawmakers had passed the Flag Protection Act, which made it illegal to deface or harm the flag in any way. But in a 5 to 4 decision the following year, the Supreme Court said that the government "may not prohibit the expression of an idea simply because society finds the idea offensive or disagreeable."[10] In other words, even though it's in poor taste to mutilate the flag, people still have the right to express their ideas in this way if they choose. If the government denies them this right, it violates the First Amendment to the Constitution, which provides for freedom of speech.

On the Court at that time was Justice Antonin Scalia, a conservative and a close friend of Ruth Ginsburg's who had once served with her on the appeals court. Scalia attended a dinner party at the Ginsburgs' house shortly after the flag-burning decision. In the case, he had voted with the majority, in favor of striking down the Flag Protection Act. Now, as he waited for dinner, Scalia sat down at the Ginsburgs' piano and began to play, "You're a Grand Old Flag."

The conservative Scalia's friendship with the Ginsburgs troubled liberals as rumors of Ruth's possible nomination for Supreme Court justice spread. Still, they welcomed the possibility of having two women on the High Court. If nominated and approved, Ginsburg would join Justice Sandra Day O'Connor, the first female justice, who had served since 1981. But liberals weren't the only ones voicing concern over Ginsburg. Conservatives, too, had reasons to worry. They feared that, after all her years supporting the ACLU and women's causes, she would side with the Court's liberal justices, like John Paul Stevens.

And yet there was one thing about Ruth Bader Ginsburg on which both sides agreed; that was her talent as a consensus builder. Throughout the

1980s and early 1990s, the Supreme Court (like the appeals court) had been divided in some of its decisions. When the High Court's votes were close, like the 5 to 4 decision on the Flag Protection Act, it meant that the justices had had a hard time reaching a consensus, or agreement. Failure to agree on issues tended to erode the strength of the Court's decisions. A close vote sent a message to the American people and to the lower courts: "Well, here is our decision, but it could very easily have gone the other way." Ginsburg herself believed that bitter disagreement among judges or justices over an issue weakened "the respect accorded to court [decisions]."[11]

Liberals and conservatives alike felt that Ruth Ginsburg could help the Court reach agreement when the justices were divided on an issue. "Her preference for strong majority opinions should . . . be a blessing,"[12] said one source. Court watchers hoped she could help the justices understand one another's views and reach strong if not unanimous agreement. During times of tough decision making, they believed, Ginsburg would act as a bridge builder. President Clinton recognized this as one of her most important qualities. As he went about the process of considering nominees for the important position of justice, the president looked to Ruth Bader Ginsburg as "a force for consensus building on the Supreme Court, just as she has been on the Court of Appeals, so that our judges can become an instrument of our common unity in the expression of their fidelity [faithfulness] to the Constitution."[13]

Chapter / Eight

A Member of the "Brethren"

After her many years of service to the sisterhood, arguing strongly for women's rights, Ruth Ginsburg's name was now being spoken in connection with the brotherhood. For years, the austere, astute justices of the Supreme Court had been known as the "Brethren." In their long black robes and oak-paneled offices, these professional brothers were the highest-ranking judges in the country. Until the confirmation of Sandra Day O'Connor in 1981, the Court had been a man's world. Was there room among the Brethren for a second sister?

At first, there didn't appear to be. In the final days before the nomination, two men were still the preferred choices. President Clinton seemed to favor Interior Secretary Bruce Babbitt, but there were problems with his nomination. Environmentalists, particularly in the western states, didn't want Babbitt pulled away from his post in the Interior Department, where he was a strong supporter of proper land use. Republicans questioned whether Babbitt's legal experience and knowledge of law were solid enough to qualify him for Supreme Court duty. Judge Stephen Breyer then became Clinton's top choice. The president invited Breyer for lunch, and the two had lengthy discussions about the Supreme Court position. But soon there were reports that Breyer had failed to pay taxes on a household employee. The president could not risk nominating a person with a single flaw on his record, and so Breyer's name was dropped for the time being (although he would later become the nation's 108th Supreme Court justice). It was then, just thirty-six hours before he would select his nominee, that Clinton turned his attention to Ruth Bader Ginsburg.

Did this mean that Ginsburg was a last-minute, third-rate pick, considered only after the president's top choices failed? Not at all. "Judge Ginsburg is a very solid choice," said a Princeton University scholar who studies the performance of presidents. If Clinton had selected her at the beginning, "I am sure everyone would have applauded."[1] Even before he was elected, Clinton had promised that any judge he appointed "would have an expansive view of the right to privacy and a woman's right to choose."[2] Although he had met Ruth Ginsburg only twice, he knew that she supported these two important rights.

Certainly there was no question of Ginsburg's legal experience or knowledge of the law keeping her from serving on the nation's highest court. As far back as 1976, *Columbia Law Review* reported that "her name was mentioned whenever seers tried to [predict] the first woman Supreme Court justice."[3]

Ginsburg had no skeletons hiding in her closets to kill her nomination at the last minute. In reporting their tax payments, *Time* magazine said, "the Ginsburgs appear blameless. . . . Martin was able to show records, in meticulous, Manila-folder order, of Social Security payments for everyone who had so much as touched a dishrag in their household."[4] (Ruth maintains it was she who kept the records!)

Ruth Ginsburg was a candidate whom both the Democrats and Republicans could accept. Her name, said one news report, "is drawing grudging praise from both liberals and conservatives." "It may be that not everyone is enthusiastic about every aspect of her record," said Marcia Greenberger of the National Women's Law Center, "but most people can find something they like."[5] Even many usually conservative business leaders supported Ginsburg's nomination. "She harbors no [dislike for] Corporate America," said one Washington lawyer. *Business Week* magazine called her "neither a conservative ideologue nor a wild-eyed radical."[6] The American Bar Association, an organization of lawyers and judges, gave Ginsburg its highest rating to serve on the Court.

Only the extremists and radicals seemed to object. Phyllis Schlafly, head of the highly conservative Eagle Forum, a group strongly against the feminist movement, accused Ginsburg of trying to "get rid of all laws that protect women as women, wives and mothers." Schlafly claimed Ginsburg's view "teaches women to believe they are oppressed, mistreated, treated like slaves" and that "having a baby is temporarily disabling like breaking a leg." On the other side, superliberals said Ginsburg didn't go far enough in her fight for equal rights. "Women are in an economic and power underclass," said a feminist law professor at Harvard University. "We need [laws] that recognize that women are differently situated."[7]

But for most people, Ruth Bader Ginsburg was what President Clinton called the perfect choice. He wasted no time in coming to a decision. On Saturday, June 12, 1993, Clinton aides called the Ginsburgs, who were about to attend a wedding in Vermont, and asked them to return to Washington the next morning. This time there was no room in the schedule for the president to lunch with the candidate, as he had with Judge Breyer. But that was probably a good thing, Martin pointed out, for Ruth eats so slowly and takes such small bites that "they might still be eating."[8]

Instead, Clinton met with Ginsburg for a ninety-minute interview in a drawing room on the second floor of the White House. Ruth replied shyly when the president asked why he should choose her for the position. "I never thought I'd be here," she admitted, "sitting in front of the president of the United States talking about whether I should be on the Supreme Court."[9]

The president had made up his mind. Ruth Bader Ginsburg would be his nominee; he would announce his decision the next day. One of the longest nominating processes in Supreme Court history had finally come to an end. And "when it was over," wrote the *New York Times*, "the sound [coming] from the capital was not 'Wow,' but 'Phew.'"[10] No one was more pleased with the president's choice than Martin Ginsburg, who had worked hard to ensure his wife's nomination. Martin even asked well-known women and professors to write letters to President Clinton assuring him that Judge Ginsburg did support the abortion rights granted in *Roe v. Wade*.

The next day, June 14, the nomination was set

Husband Martin, in the Ginsburg's Watergate apartment in Washington, D.C.

to take place in the Rose Garden of the White House. Gathered in the garden were family members, attorneys, members of Congress, and friends. The Ginsburgs' daughter, Jane, who was in

Australia, called her mother shortly before the nomination to remind her of an entry in her high school yearbook. The yearbook had listed Jane's ambition, "to see her mother appointed to the Supreme Court," and added, "If necessary, Jane will appoint her." Turning to Clinton during her accep-tance speech, Ruth remarked, "Jane is so pleased, Mr. President, that you did it instead."[11]

In his nomination, President Clinton explained that he had selected Ruth Ginsburg for three rea-sons. First, he said, she was one of America's finest judges. Next he spoke of her many years of service to women's rights, saying she had "compiled a truly historic record of achievement in the finest tradi-tions of American law and citizenship." The third reason, Clinton said, was his belief that "in the years ahead, she will be . . . a force for consensus-building on the Supreme Court."

The president called Ruth Ginsburg's life "a remarkable record of distinction and achievement both professional and personal." He quoted from an article she had written that said, "The greatest figures of the American judiciary have been inde-pendent [thinkers] with open but not empty minds—individuals willing to listen and to learn." Ginsburg must be included among those great fig-ures, the president said. "And," he added, "she has done all of this . . . while raising a family with her husband, Marty."[12]

Ruth's family is indeed a credit to her. Each of the Ginsburgs has a record of hard work and achievement. Martin, a law professor at Georgetown University Law Center, is one of the nation's foremost tax lawyers, counting among his clients billionaire Ross Perot. After earning a college degree in the arts, Jane studied law at Harvard and eventually followed her mother into teaching at Columbia University. The Ginsburgs' son, James, who attended law school in Chicago, is a producer of classical CDs.

In their leisure time, the Ginsburgs share a passion for music, which for Ruth is centered in the opera. "She would cry at *The Marriage of Figaro* [a comedy] if she had the chance,"[13] jokes James. Ruth also likes watching old movies and reading the mysteries of Amanda Cross and Dorothy L. Sayers. Waterskiing and horseback riding are two of her favorite sports, along with golf, which she plays with Martin. (She considers her game too poor to play with anyone else.) A friend once compared Ginsburg's golfing style (she's left-handed, but learned to play with right-handed clubs) to her mixture of liberal and conservative views in the courtroom. Ruth played golf like she decided legal cases, the friend observed, "aiming left, swinging right and hitting down the middle."[14] She disputes

Jane Ginsburg presents her mother with an award at Harvard Law School.

the friend's third observation.

Even in their leisure time, work is never far away. Once while the Ginsburgs were vacationing in Israel, Martin sat by the pool at the King David

Hotel, working on a law review article he was writing, while Ruth rushed off to a debate on the position of women under different legal systems. Their
professional lives and their personal interests are
closely tied, and they bring the same high standards
to each.

Said President Clinton in closing his nominating speech in the Rose Garden, "If, as I believe, the
measure of a person's values can best be measured
by examining the life the person lives, then Judge
Ginsburg's values are the very ones that represent
the best in America."[15] There was much applause.

Ruth's acceptance speech followed. "I am
indebted to so many for this extraordinary chance
and challenge," she said, praising her family and
remembering her mother, Celia Amster Bader. She
thanked the president for the confidence he had
placed in her and then quoted from an article
about Oliver Wendell Holmes, one of the nation's
greatest Supreme Court justices. "When a
modern . . . judge is confronted with a hard case,"
the article said, "Holmes is at her side with three
gentle reminders." The first is to be honest in
reviewing the laws that pertain to a case and in
selecting the right course of action. The second is
to respect the decision of the majority. And the
third is a commitment to respect individual opinions, even when they disagree with the majority. If

confirmed, Ginsburg promised, she would work "to
the best of my ability for the advancement of the
law in the service of society."[16]

After her nomination, the Senate Judiciary
Committee, a specially selected group of U.S. senators, held confirmation hearings. The hearings
began July 20. During three days of testimony, the
senators asked Ginsburg questions about her back-
ground, her views, and her stand on certain issues.
At the same time, reporters and investigators
searched Ginsburg's past to see if any events in her
life might make her unfit for this important position. With her usual direct, honest approach,
Ginsburg told key senators before the hearings
began, "I hope my answers please the Senate
Judiciary Committee, but in the end, I am what I
am."[17]

On the first day of the hearings, she made it
clear that she was not going to predict how she
would vote on particular issues. "I come to this pro-
ceeding to be judged as a judge. . . . It would be
wrong for me to say or preview . . . how I would cast
my vote on questions the Supreme Court may be
called upon to decide."[18] And although she was
very clear about her stand on abortion rights, she
gave no clue as to her views on the death penalty
or other major issues. Ginsburg said she would
make up her mind by examining the law, analyzing

William Rehnquist (right), chief justice of the Supreme Court, gives the oaths of office to the nation's 107th justice, Ruth Bader Ginsburg, while President Bill Clinton looks on. Martin Ginsburg holds the Bible.

precedent, and discussing the facts of the case with the other justices. Always, she stressed, she would encourage the Court to reach a consensus, not a narrowly split decision.

When the hearings were over, the Senate voted on whether to approve President Clinton's nominee. The decision came on August 3, 1993, in a nearly unanimous vote: 96 in favor, only 3 opposed. It was the smoothest confirmation in many years, quite different from the controversy that had surrounded the appointment of Justice Clarence Thomas, nominated by President George Bush two years earlier. President Clinton said he was proud to have nominated a person who, during the confirmation hearings, showed "tremendous intellect, integrity, comprehension of the law and compassion for the concerns of all Americans."[19] On August 10, 1993, Ruth Bader Ginsburg took the oaths of office that made her the 107th justice, only the second woman and the first Jew since 1969 to serve on the Supreme Court of the United States of America.

Chapter / Nine

The Nation's Second Female Justice

"The Supreme Court's new term is off to a roaring start," reported Alan Dershowitz in early October 1993. Dershowitz, an outspoken Harvard law professor and national newspaper columnist, had been one of Ruth Ginsburg's harshest critics when she was a nominee. Now he seemed to be softening his view. "In her first hour on the bench," Dershowitz noted, "she asked 17 questions—more than Justices Clarence Thomas and David Souter together asked during their first weeks on the court."[1]

It was clear from the start that the nation's newest female justice was not going to be a wallflower. Ruth Ginsburg entered the Court prepared to ask questions, talk with fellow justices, and speak or write her mind on the issues put before her. Her black judicial robe (all justices must purchase their own) hung heavy on her shoulders. She took her new duties very seriously, making it clear that she intended to let the Constitution, the laws of the land, and the facts of each case guide her in her decisions. She would not be swayed by public opinion or by loyalty to those who had helped her build her career.

When she entered the marbled halls of the Supreme Court, across the street from the Capitol, Ginsburg (like each justice) was assigned a five-room suite called a chambers. The Court's active justices have always occupied chambers on the first floor, but Ginsburg decided to locate on the second floor, in the offices used by retired Justice Thurgood Marshall before his death in 1993. She preferred this location, she said, because "the space is light, airy, and quiet. And there is something special about being in the place where Justice Marshall worked. . . . No other lawyer in . . . modern times used his talent to better advantage than Justice Marshall did."[2]

Justice Ginsburg's chambers overlook a court-yard where Supreme Court staff members some-times gather for lunch, sitting on the stone benches or around patio tables. On pleasant afternoons, law clerks sometimes work outside under large, shady umbrellas. In keeping with the light, airy chambers she chose, Ginsburg decided not to use the Court's heavy leather chairs and other furnishings that gave her the feeling of being in a men's club. Instead, she outfitted her offices in modern furniture made of chrome and glass. Along one wall are oak bookcases filled with the justice's most needed volumes, as well as photos of her family. On the walls hang pieces of modern art, one of her strong interests. Her large desk, made of mahogany with brass trim, was built in the Supreme Court carpentry shop. On days when she works in the courtroom—"on the bench"—she sits in a large black leather-upholstered chair.

The justice's staff includes two secretaries, a messenger, and four law clerks—the position she herself never received as a newly graduated law student. Apparently recalling those days and her own difficulties as a young lawyer, Ginsburg allowed one of her clerks to set flexible working hours, something never before done at the Court. The clerk was a young man who had clerked for Ginsburg at the appeals court. They had set the flexible schedule then because the clerk needed to be at home with his children while his wife worked. "This is my dream of the way the world should be," said the justice. "When fathers take equal responsibility for the care of their children, that's when women will truly be liberated."[3]

The newest member of the Supreme Court is

called the junior justice, and that person is responsible for certain chores and duties that senior
justices do not have. While she was junior justice,
Ginsburg was required to keep track of her colleagues' votes on selecting cases for Court
review and to report the justices' decisions to
the clerk of the Court. It was also her duty to act
as doorkeeper when the nine justices gathered
for weekly private meetings. It was the job of the
junior justice to carry and receive messages from
the staff outside the oak-paneled conference room
to the proper justices within. Responsibility for
organizing the justices' Christmas party fell to
her during her rookie term. But the role of junior
justice would be Ginsburg's for just one year. By
the time her second term on the Court began,
Stephen Breyer had been named to replace
the retiring Harry Blackmun. If confirmed by the
Senate, Breyer would become the new junior
justice.

Ruth Ginsburg settled into her first term
with a warm welcome from her fellow justices and
a big hug from colleague Sandra Day O'Connor.
Already Court watchers were wondering how
Ginsburg would vote on certain issues. When the
Supreme Court came to key decisions, would
she lean to the liberal left, sit in the middle on the
"centrist fence," or vote with the conservative

right? "She's tough to pigeon-hole,"[4] remarked one reporter. On the subject of criminal law, for example, Ginsburg supports the government's duty to uphold the law, but she also supports the right of the defendants to a fair trial. While liberals often side with the defendants and conservatives usually support government authority, Ginsburg believes that the two sides should have a full and fair voice.

Likewise on affirmative action—the move to give members of minority groups a boost in education and the job market. Here, too, Ginsburg walks a middle ground. Even though she supports help for the disadvantaged, she looks for "equality, not favoritism"[5] on issues involving affirmative action. A person should not be given advantages just because he or she represents a minority group, Ginsburg insists.

During her first months at the Court, while the job was new, "I found myself chained to my desk,"[6] Ginsburg reported. One area that consumed much more of her time than she had imagined was the death penalty, an issue that has been hotly debated over the last twenty years. In 1972 the Supreme Court ruled that the death penalty, as it was being carried out at that time, was unconstitutional. But during the next four years, states passed laws that made capital punishment

legal within the framework of the Constitution. However, the subject of the death penalty continues to be a point of major concern for attorneys, judges, and civil rights groups. "I had no idea," Ginsburg admitted, "how many hours the Justices spend dealing with death cases. . . . Every capital case is on the discuss list, and each Justice's chambers is alert for each pre-execution vigil."[7]

On the docket during Ginsburg's first term were several controversial cases. In one, the Court was asked to decide whether a person claiming sexual harassment had to prove that she (or he) had suffered "psychological injury." The case involved Theresa Harris, an employee at Forklift Systems, who claimed she had been harassed by her boss. Just twenty-seven days after argument—a short time for a major case—the justices unanimously agreed that sexual harassment included any behavior that made the workplace "hostile or abusive" to a "reasonable person."[8] Victims did not have to prove that they had suffered psychological injury. Justice Sandra Day O'Connor wrote the opinion in the Harris case; Ginsburg, even though she agreed, wrote a separate opinion. In it, she reminded the Court (and the public) that the issue of whether gender discrimination should be judged as harshly as racial discrimination "remains an open question."[9]

The nation's newest female Supreme Court justice at work

In addition to the sexual harassment issue,
the justices heard cases dealing with everything
from job discrimination to trash disposal. They
considered the claim of NOW, the National
Organization for Women, that antiabortion pro-
testers were part of a nationwide conspiracy to
shut down abortion clinics by illegal means and
activities. Randall Terry and other pro-life leaders
were upset by the Supreme Court's unanimous
decision that seemed to strengthen the position
of abortion rights supporters. "This is the iron heel
of government crushing protest and dissent,"[10]
said Terry.

The Supreme Court questioned whether
home owners had a right to display political slogans
in the windows of their homes. Justices tackled
the question of whether boundary lines in election
districts could be changed to ensure an occasional
win at the polls for minority groups. In a case
brought by the Turner Broadcasting System, the
Court was asked to decide whether Congress could
require operators of cable television companies to
devote certain channels to programmers that were
favored by Congress. Would such a ruling violate
the First Amendment, which provides for freedom
of the press?

Through each of these cases, Court watchers
wondered, "Will Ruth Ginsburg make a differ-

ence?" It was still too early to tell, and too soon to pin a conservative, centrist, or liberal label on Ginsburg. It would be a long time, if ever, before anyone could predict Ruth Bader Ginsburg's voting habits. What people wanted to see were signs that she could pull together the Supreme Court when it was divided on issues, just as she had done on the appeals court. This time, even Alan Dershowitz seemed hopeful. "The key to the new [consensus]-building may well lie with the court's two women," he suggested. "This term may mark the first time in American history that a branch of our government has been so influenced by women."[11]

Ginsburg realized that the task of consensus building would be harder to accomplish on the Supreme Court than it had been on the appeals court. There, only three of the twelve judges usually rule on a case, but at the Supreme Court, all nine justices participate. Working with the smaller number on the appeals court made it easier to reach agreement. Observed Ginsburg, "I can appreciate why unanimity is so much harder to achieve in Supreme Court judgments. . . . It is ever so much easier to have a conversation among three than among nine."[12]

The greatest challenge facing the Supreme Court today, says Ginsburg, "is to preserve the remarkable role it has had in U.S. society. It's like no other court in the world. . . . Its position depends on the acceptance [that] its judgments receive."[13] Maintaining the respect that the U.S. Supreme Court has built up over two centuries is a tremendous challenge to its justices, Ginsburg acknowledges.

But although the Supreme Court must remain a strong and respected institution, none of the courts should become the leaders of social change, Ginsburg warns. They must not set new styles or trends for Americans' behavior. When judges or justices make decisions that are too far ahead of the times and trends, the public loses faith in them, Ginsburg explains. This was one of her complaints in *Roe v. Wade*. The idea of legalized abortion was too new in 1973 for the Supreme Court to set specific rules on how or when it could be carried out. It should have been enough for the Court to rule against the Texas law and let the states decide, over time, just what regulations would govern abortion.

The judicial branch of government should not tread too heavily on the executive and legislative branches, says Ginsburg. Justices must remember that they are not the ones who make the laws; that is the job of the legislative branch. Nor do they enforce the laws; that power belongs to the executive branch. The responsibility of the judicial branch is to interpret or explain the laws. And although the Court has the power to declare a law unconstitutional, Ginsburg believes that the nine justices should not be too quick to strike down rules that several hundred lawmakers in Congress have passed. By claiming too much power, the judicial branch puts itself out of balance with the other two arms of government. "Most urgently needed," she says, "is a clear recognition by all branches of government that in a representative democracy, important . . . questions should be confronted, debated and resolved by *elected* officials."[14]

Life at the Supreme Court seems to suit Ruth Ginsburg. "I have never worked any place where there has been a greater esprit [enthusiasm]. There's a notable 'We want to be helpful' attitude,"[15] which she says is very different from many workplaces, particularly within the government. But her new job doesn't keep her constantly tied to Washington or the Supreme Court building. During her first year, she traveled to India with Justice Antonin Scalia, where they gave talks to lawyers and judges. When their business was completed, the two took a side trip to Jaipur, the "pink city," where they went for a ride on an elephant. Back in Washington during a break from the Court,

Ginsburg and Scalia—both opera lovers—dressed up in seventeenth-century wigs and costumes and sat on the stage during a Washington Opera performance, as part of a pretend audience.

Moving to the Supreme Court was not as great a change for Ginsburg as it often is for new justices, because she had spent the previous thirteen years carrying out many of the same duties—reading briefs, writing opinions, and deciding issues. Yet, when asked if becoming a Supreme Court justice had changed her life, she responded, "Yes, indubitably, yes!" To her surprise, she is now recognized by strangers in public places. Before, she recalls, "no one would have paid any attention to my compulsion to save time." But recently someone reported to Martin, "Your wife reads her mail by flashlight in the movies." It's true; Ruth admits, "I don't care much for commercials and previews."[16] She has since received several pocket flashlights from well-wishers.

The nation's newest woman justice is a perfectionist, a professional, a person who believes strongly in herself and in the justice system of the United States of America. At her nominating speech in the Rose Garden, President Clinton told the crowd, "A Supreme Court justice should have the heart and spirit, the talent and discipline, the knowledge, common sense, and wisdom to translate the hopes of the American people [into a lasting body of law]."[17] Ruth Ginsburg is just that sort of person. She lives by her belief that a good judge must have strong confidence in herself. "It's important to be secure in your own judgment, to be ready to make decisions and not look back. A judge should have the attitude, 'I can resolve this as well as, or probably better than, the next person . . . and I'm not going to worry about [my decision] constantly after I've made it.'"[18]

Certainly education, hard work, and determination have been the major forces behind Ruth Ginsburg's accomplishments. But fate figured into her successes, too, she insists. "I had the great good fortune to be born at the right place in the right time, to be born in the 30's instead of the 20's, and in the United States of America. I never could have [accomplished my goals] in any other country, in any other legal system, at any earlier time. . . . At no prior age could one get across the message that women and men should be equal citizens, equal participants in community affairs."[19]

Regardless of how history looks back on her service as a justice, Ruth Bader Ginsburg has already made a tremendous contribution to her country. Before ever being named to the High

Court, she had made a place for herself in American history as a pioneer in women's rights. But Ginsburg sees her successes in a broader light. What she calls her most significant work is "the advancement of equal opportunity and responsibility for women and men in all fields of human endeavor."[20]

/Chapter Notes

Chapter 1

1. President's nominating speech, *New York Times*, June 15, 1993.
2. Ginsburg's acceptance speech, *New York Times*, June 15, 1993.
3. David Margolick, "Trial by Adversity Shapes Jurist's Outlook," *New York Times*, June 25, 1993.
4. Elinor Porter Swiger, *Women Lawyers at Work* (New York: Julian Messner, 1978), p. 56.
5. Ibid., p. 55.

Chapter 2

1. Margolick, "Trial by Adversity."
2. Aaron Epstein and Mary Otto, "Ginsburg Has Pressed for Equality for All," *Sunday Rutland Herald and Sunday Times Argus*, July 4, 1993.
3. Margolick, "Trial by Adversity."
4. Epstein and Otto, "Ginsburg Has Pressed for Equality."
5. Jeanette Friedman, "Ruth Bader Ginsburg: A Rare Interview," *Lifestyles*, March 1994, p. 12.
6. Lynn Gilbert and Gaylen Moore, *Particular Passions: Talks with Women Who Have Shaped Our Times* (New York: Crown Books, 1981), p. 156.

7. Ibid.
8. Neil A. Lewis, "Rejected as Clerk, Now Headed for Bench," *New York Times*, June 15, 1993.
9. Ibid.
10. "Biographical Data" (Washington, D.C.: Public Affairs Office, U.S. Supreme Court, 1993).
11. Ginsburg, acceptance speech.
12. Margaret Carlson, "The Law According to Ruth," *Time*, June 28, 1993, p. 38.

Chapter 3

1. Gilbert and Moore, *Particular Passions*, p. 157.
2. Ibid., p. 156.
3. Swiger, *Women Lawyers at Work*, p. 55.
4. Gilbert and Moore, *Particular Passions*, pp. 157–158.
5. Ibid., p. 158.
6. Margolick, "Trial by Adversity."
7. Ibid.
8. Swiger, *Women Lawyers at Work*, p. 55.
9. Gilbert and Moore, *Particular Passions*, p. 157.
10. Margolick, "Trial by Adversity."
11. Ibid.
12. Ibid.
13. Swiger, *Women Lawyers at Work*, p. 55.

Chapter 4

1. Carlson, "The Law According to Ruth," p. 38.
2. Gilbert and Moore, *Particular Passions*, p. 158.
3. Swiger, *Women Lawyers at Work*, p. 58.
4. Carlson, "The Law According to Ruth," p. 38.
5. Margolick, "Trial by Adversity."
6. David A. Kaplan and Bob Cohn, "A Frankfurter, Not a Hot Dog," *Newsweek*, June 28, 1993, p. 29.
7. Gilbert and Moore, *Particular Passions*, p. 158.
8. Margolick, "Trial by Adversity."
9. Gilbert and Moore, *Particular Passions*, p. 158.
10. Ibid.
11. Swiger, *Women Lawyers at Work*, p. 62.
12. Margolick, "Trial by Adversity."
13. Swiger, *Women Lawyers at Work*, p. 60.
14. Ibid., p. 61.
15. Gilbert and Moore, *Particular Passions*, p. 159.
16. Ibid., p. 153.
17. Swiger, *Women Lawyers at Work*, p. 61.
18. Ibid., p. 69.

Chapter 5

1. Ted Yanak and Pam Cornelison, *The Great American History Fact-Finder* (Boston: Houghton-Mifflin, 1993), p. 170.

2. Margolick, "Trial by Adversity."
3. Bill Hewitt, "Feeling Supreme," *People,* June 28, 1993, p. 50.
4. John W. Wright, ed., *The Universal Almanac* (Kansas City, Mo.: Andrews and McNeel, 1989), p. 47.
5. Gilbert and Moore, *Particular Passions,* p. 153.
6. Ibid.
7. Ruth B. Cowan, "Women's Rights Through Litigation," *Columbia Human Rights Law Review* 8, no. 1 (Spring-Summer 1976): p. 383.
8. Ibid., p. 392.
9. Lewis, "Rejected as Clerk."
10. Cowan, "Women's Rights Through Litigation" p. 394.
11. Lewis, "Rejected as Clerk."
12. Swiger, *Women Lawyers at Work,* p. 52.
13. Epstein and Otto, "Ginsburg Has Pressed for Equality for All," p. C4.
14. Lewis, "Rejected as Clerk."
15. Kaplan and Cohn, "A Frankfurter, Not a Hot Dog," p. 29.
16. Margolick, "Trial by Adversity."
17. Swiger, *Women Lawyers at Work,* p. 56.
18. Cowan, "Women's Rights Through Litigation," p. 397.
19. Ibid., p. 399.
20. Swiger, *Women Lawyers at Work,* p. 65.

21. Epstein and Otto, "Ginsburg Has Pressed for Equality for All," p. C4.
22. Hewitt, "Feeling Supreme," p. 50.

Chapter 6

1. Margolick, "Trial by Adversity."
2. Swiger, *Women Lawyers at Work*, p. 64.
3. *Almanac of the Federal Judiciary*, vol. 2 (Englewood Cliffs, N.J.: Prentice Hall Law & Business, 1993), Supreme Court, p. 6.
4. Catherine Yang, "Ruth Bader Ginsburg: 'So Principled, She's Unpredictable,'" *Business Week*, June 28, 1993, p. 30.
5. "Ginsburg Says Constitution Will Guide Her," *Rocky Mountain News*, July 21, 1993.
6. Steven V. Roberts, "Two Lives of Ruth Bader Ginsburg," *U.S. News & World Report*, June 28, 1993, p. 26.
7. Kaplan and Cohn, "A Frankfurter, Not a Hot Dog," p. 29.
8. Roberts, "Two Lives of Ruth Bader Ginsburg," p. 26.
9. Ruth Bader Ginsburg, "Dissenting Opinion in *Goldman v. Secretary of Defense*," *New York Times*, June 15, 1993.
10. Mary Deibel, "Senate's Spotlight on Ginsburg,"

Rocky Mountain News, July 19, 1993.

Chapter 7
1. Roberts, "Two Lives of Ruth Bader Ginsburg," p. 28.
2. Carlson, "The Law According to Ruth," p. 38.
3. Roberts, "Two Lives of Ruth Bader Ginsburg," p. 28.
4. *Almanac of the Federal Judiciary*, vol. 2, p. 6.
5. Mickey Kaus, "Nominee's Case Calls Her Caution into Question," *Rocky Mountain News*, June 30, 1993.
6. Swiger, *Women Lawyers at Work*, pp. 57–58.
7. Kenneth T. Walsh, "The 'Elastic Presidency,'" *U.S. News & World Report*, June 28, 1993, p. 20.
8. "Judge Ginsburg Nominated to Replace White on Supreme Court," *Facts on File*, June 17, 1993, p. 443.
9. Thomas L. Friedman, "The 11th-Hour Scramble," *New York Times*, June 15, 1993.
10. "Supreme Court Strikes Down New Flag-Burning Law," *Facts on File*, June 15, 1990, p. 436.
11. "Scoping Ginsburg," *The Nation*, July 12, 1993, p. 51.

12. Yang, "Ruth Bader Ginsburg: 'So Principled, She's Unpredictable,'" p. 30.
13. Jeanette Friedman, "Ruth Bader Ginsburg: A Rare Interview," p. 13.

Chapter 8

1. Thomas L. Friedman, "The 11th-Hour Scramble."
2. Mickey Kaus, "Roe to Ruin," *The New Republic*, April 12, 1993, p. 6.
3. Cowan, "Women's Rights Through Litigation," p. 384.
4. Carlson, "The Law According to Ruth," p. 38.
5. Deibel, "Senate's Spotlight on Ginsburg."
6. Yang, "Ruth Bader Ginsburg: 'So Principled, She's Unpredictable,'" p. 30.
7. Epstein and Otto, "Ginsburg Has Pressed for Equality."
8. Margolick, "Trial by Adversity."
9. Walsh, "The 'Elastic Presidency,'" p. 20.
10. Thomas L. Friedman, "The 11th-Hour Scramble."
11. Ginsburg, acceptance speech.
12. Clinton, nominating speech.
13. Margolick, "Trial by Adversity."
14. Ibid.

15. Clinton, nominating speech.
16. Ginsburg, acceptance speech.
17. Deibel, "Senate's Spotlight on Ginsburg."
18. "Ginsburg Says Constitution Will Guide Her."
19. "Senate Approves Ginsburg for Court," *Rocky Mountain News*, August 4, 1993.

Chapter 9

1. Alan Dershowitz, "We Deserve to Know What Goes on Behind High Court's Doors," *Rocky Mountain News*, October 11, 1993.
2. Toni House and Kathleen Arberg, "And Then There Were Two," *Docket Sheet of the Supreme Court of the United States* 30, no. 1 (Fall 1993): p. 8.
3. Ibid.
4. Deibel, "Senate's Spotlight on Ginsburg."
5. Roberts, "Two Lives of Ruth Bader Ginsburg," p. 28.
6. House and Arberg, "And Then There Were Two," p. 3.
7. Ibid.
8. David A. Kaplan, "Take Down the Girlie Calendars," *Newsweek*, November 22, 1993, p. 34.

9. Ibid.

10. Tony Mauro and Mimi Hall, "Racketeering Law 'Tool' Against Clinic Violence," *USA Today*, January 25, 1994.

11. Dershowitz, "We Deserve to Know."

12. *Almanac of the Federal Judiciary*, vol. 2, p. 7.

13. Jeanette Friedman, "Ruth Bader Ginsburg: A Rare Interview," p. 15.

14. Ibid.

15. House and Arberg, "And Then There Were Two," p. 1.

16. Ibid., p.3.

17. Clinton, nominating speech.

18. House and Arberg, "And Then There Were Two," p. 3.

19. Ibid., p. 8.

20. Ellen Goodman, "Ginsburg Heralds Arrival of the 'Conservative Feminist,'" p. 35A.

Appendix
Ruth Bader Ginsburg: A Time Line

March 15, 1933—Ruth Joan Bader is born in Brooklyn, New York.

June 1950—Celia Bader, Ruth's mother, dies of cancer at age forty-seven, one day before Ruth's high school graduation.

September 1950—Ruth enters college as a freshman at Cornell University in Ithaca, New York.

June 23, 1954—Ruth Bader marries Martin David Ginsburg the same month that she graduates from Cornell University.

July 21, 1955—The Ginsburgs' first child, Jane Carol, is born in Fort Sill, Oklahoma, where Martin is serving in the army.

September 1956—Ruth enters Harvard Law School as one of only nine women in a class of more than four hundred. Martin begins his second year as a law student there.

1958—Martin Ginsburg graduates from Harvard Law School and accepts a job with a New York law firm. The family moves to New York, and

Ruth transfers to Columbia University Law School.

June 1959—Ruth Bader Ginsburg graduates at the top of her class from Columbia University Law School in New York.

1959–1961—Ruth works as a law clerk to Edmund L. Palmieri, U.S. District Court judge for the Southern District of New York.

1961–1963—Ginsburg travels to Sweden, living a total of six months in that country, as a research associate and later associate director of the Columbia Law School Project on International Procedure.

1963—Ginsburg serves on the faculty as a professor of law at Rutgers University in Newark, New Jersey, where she will remain until 1972.

September 8, 1965—The Ginsburgs' second child, James Steven, is born.

1971—Ginsburg helps to launch the Women's Rights Project, a division of the American Civil Liberties Union.

1972—Ginsburg accepts a part-time teaching position at Columbia University Law School in New York, a job she will hold until 1980. During the same period, she also serves as legal counsel to the Women's Rights Project.

June 30, 1980—Ruth Bader Ginsburg takes the oath of office as a judge on the United States Court of Appeals, serving on the District of Columbia Circuit.

1981—Sandra Day O'Connor is appointed by President Ronald Reagan as the first woman justice on the United States Supreme Court.

June 14, 1993—Ruth Bader Ginsburg is nominated by President Bill Clinton for the position of Supreme Court justice, to replace the retiring Justice Byron White.

July 20, 1993—The Senate Judiciary Committee begins hearings on the nomination of Ruth Ginsburg as Supreme Court justice.

August 10, 1993—Ruth Bader Ginsburg takes the oaths of office that make her the 107th justice, and only the second woman, to serve on the United States Supreme Court.

October 4, 1993—Ginsburg begins her first term as a Supreme Court justice.

/ Selected Bibliography

BOOKS

Almanac of the Federal Judiciary, vol. 2. Englewood Cliffs, N.J.: Prentice Hall Law & Business, 1993.

Coy, Harold. *The Supreme Court*. New York: Franklin Watts, 1981.

Gilbert, Lynn, and Gaylen Moore. *Particular Passions: Talks with Women Who Have Shaped Our Times*. New York: Crown Books, 1981.

Ginsburg, Ruth Bader. "Biographical Data." Washington, D.C.: Public Affairs Office, U.S. Supreme Court, 1993.

Green, Carol. *The Supreme Court*. New York: Regensteiner, 1985.

Swiger, Elinor Porter. *Women Lawyers at Work*. New York: Julian Messner, 1978.

Wright, John W., ed. *The Universal Almanac*. Kansas City, Mo.: Andrews and McMeel, 1989.

Yanak, Ted, and Pam Cornelison. *The Great American History Fact-Finder*. Boston: Houghton-Mifflin, 1993.

PERIODICALS

Business Week. June 28, 1993, p. 30.

Columbia Human Rights Law Review 8, no. 1 (Spring–Summer 1976): pp. 373–404.

Docket Sheet of the Supreme Court of the United States 30, no. 1 (Fall 1993): pp. 1–8.

Facts on File, June 15, 1990, p. 436; June 17, 1993, pp. 443–444.

Kiplinger Washington Letter, September 17, 1993, p. 3.

Lifestyles, March 1994, pp. 6–13.

The Nation, July 12, 1993, pp. 51–52; August 23/30, 1993, pp. 197–198; October 25, 1993, pp. 452–454.

New Republic, April 12, 1993, pp. 6, 21, 24–26; July 5, 1993, p. 7; August 16, 1993, p. 10.

Newsweek, June 28, 1993, p. 29; November 22, 1993, p. 34.

New York Times, June 15, 1993 (National): pp. A1, A11, A14, A15; June 25, 1993 (National): pp. A1, A19; June 27, 1993: pp. 1, 10.

People, June 28, 1993, pp. 49–50.

Rocky Mountain News, June 30, 1993, pp. 22A, 23A, 37A; July 19, 1993, pp. 18A, 20A; July 21, 1993, p. 3A; July 26, 1993, p. 35A; August 4, 1993, p. 3A; October 11, 1993, p. 45A.

Sunday Rutland Herald and Sunday Times Argus, July 4, 1993, p. C4.

Time, June 28, 1993, pp. 38–40.

USA Today, January 25, 1994, p. A1.

U.S. News & World Report, June 28, 1993, pp. 20–22, 24–26, 28.

/Index